STRENGTHENING DISABILITY-INCLUSIVE DEVELOPMENT

2021–2025 ROAD MAP

ASIAN DEVELOPMENT BANK

Contents

Table, Figures, and Boxes

Foreword

Around 70% of people with disabilities live in Asia and the Pacific—about 690 million people. They are among the poorest in the region and face significant challenges such as social exclusion and increased inequality as well as extreme poverty. Their number will increase as the region's population ages: more than half of all people with disabilities are over 60 years old, and by 2050 one in four people in Asia and the Pacific will be over 60.

This road map will help the Asian Development Bank (ADB) strengthen its approach to disability-inclusive development to enhance the impact of work with and for the poorest and most excluded people in the region. It was prepared as one of nine commitments ADB made in 2018 at the first Global Disability Summit alongside other international development partners. It sets out a practical pathway to greater disability inclusion in ADB projects, research, and organizational systems, and will support implementation of the bank's Strategy 2030 across operational priorities.

The road map builds on ADB's experience as a strategic partner for and investor in social inclusion, social development, gender mainstreaming, and disability-inclusive development. Its aims include supporting the active participation and empowerment of people with disabilities and increasing the capacity and knowledge of ADB staff. These activities will create the foundation for a more comprehensive and integrated approach to disability-inclusive development at ADB in the longer term.

The bank will use this road map to guide and strengthen both current and future projects involving disability-inclusive development. In Bangladesh, Mongolia, and Viet Nam, for example, ADB is supporting inclusive education for children and young people with disabilities. In Mongolia, ADB is implementing its first loan fully focused on inclusion and services for people with disabilities. Several transport and infrastructure projects that target people with disabilities are also underway in the region, including the Mumbai Metro project. In Georgia and Pakistan, ADB- assisted urban and transport programs have been influential in developing guidance on inclusive design.

Supporting the implementation of the road map will be a new disability reference group. This will include national and regional organizations of persons with disabilities and those working with people with disabilities, academics, and other experts. The reference group will play an important role in providing feedback on progress and helping to shape ADB's work in disability-inclusive development.

Disability inclusion will benefit individuals, communities, and countries across Asia and the Pacific. In all sectors there are opportunities to promote inclusion and address the challenges faced by "left-behind" groups. This road map represents a significant step forward in ADB's work to help end extreme poverty, increase prosperity, and support people in the region to improve their lives. We thank everyone who contributed their guidance, expertise, and commitment to help create it.

Woochong Um
Managing Director General
Asian Development Bank

Acknowledgments

This Road Map for Strengthening Disability Inclusive Development, 2021-2025, brings together several related pieces of work on inclusion and disability by various units within ADB under the overall guidance of Wendy Walker, chief of the Social Development Thematic Group (SDTG), with support from independent consultant on disability inclusion, Joanna Rogers, and taking more than a year of consultations both internally and with some external stakeholders.

The team wishes to specifically thank the various staff who granted interviews for the initial draft of the road map: Thomas Abell, Michael Anyala, Oliver Chapman, Arup Chatterjee, Xijie Lu, Christopher Morris, Keiko Nowacka, Patrick Osewe, Brajesh Panth, Mary Alice Rosero, Virinder Sharma, Ramola Naik Singru, Gohar Tadevosyan, Elaine Thomas, Francesco Tornieri, and Lloyd Fredrick Wright; to then SDTG Committee members Rana Hasan and Bernard Woods for their comments; other colleagues in the sector and thematic groups and other departments who provided feedback on an earlier draft: Lara Arjan, Eduardo Banzon, Ninebeth Carandang, Lisette Cipriano, Alaysa Escandor, Dorothy Geronimo, Francesca Molinaro, Irina Novikova, Jukka Tulivuori, and Hyun Joo Youn; and more colleagues during the formal interdepartmental review: Tahmeen Ahmad, Glenita Amoranto, Analyn Bravo, Jenny Yan Yee Chu, Puri Gamon, Prabhjot Khan, Martin Kroll, Jamie Leather, Sunghoon Kris Moon, Lyailya T. Nazarbekova, Gloria Paniagua, Anders Pettersson, Frances Lynette V. Sayson, Pinky Serafica, Rajeev Singh, Aiko Kikkawa Takenaka, and Milan Thomas.

Our appreciation also goes to colleagues in the Economic and Social Commission for Asia and the Pacific Srinivas Tata, director of Social Development Division, and Cai Cai, Chief of Gender Equality and Social Inclusion Section; Alex Cote, Disability and Social Protection Specialist at United Nations Children's Fund; Vicki Austin, co-founder of Global Disability Innovation Hub; Teresa Lee, advisor, Christian Blind Mission Global Inclusion Advisory Group; Abner Manlapaz, co-founder of Life Haven for Independent Living in the Philippines; Laisa Vereti, director for Operations of the Pacific Disability Forum; and Oidov Vaanchig, founder of the Mongolian startup on aids for daily living Rehtus LLC, who altogether provided insightful and detailed inputs to the draft road map.

Special thanks to Managing Director General Woochong Um, and the managements of the Sustainable Development and Climate Change Department, and the Budget, People and Management Systems Department (BPMSD) for their support. The Culture and Talent Division at BPMSD as well as the Results, Management and Aid Effectiveness Division of the Strategy, Policy and Partnerships Department played major roles during the development of the road map and will remain critical partners during implementation. This road map was approved in November 2021.

Abbreviations

ADB	–	Asian Development Bank
BPMSD	–	Budget, Personnel, and Management Systems Department, ADB
COVID-19	–	coronavirus disease
CPS	–	country partnership strategy
CRPD	–	United Nations Convention on the Rights of Persons with Disabilities
CSO	–	civil society organization
DFAT	–	Department of Foreign Affairs and Trade, Australia
DFID	–	Department for International Development, United Kingdom (former name of the Foreign, Commonwealth & Development Office, or FCDO)
DIB	–	Diversity, Inclusion, and Belonging (Framework)
DMC	–	developing member country
ESCAP	–	United Nations Economic and Social Commission for Asia and the Pacific
FCDO	–	Foreign, Commonwealth & Development Office, United Kingdom
GDIH	–	Global Disability Innovation Hub
GDP	–	gross domestic product
GLAD	–	Global Action on Disability
NGO	–	nongovernment organization
OPD	–	organization of persons with disabilities
PPFD	–	Procurement, Portfolio, and Financial Management Department, ADB
PRC	–	People's Republic of China
RRP	–	report and recommendation of the President
SDG	–	United Nations Sustainable Development Goal
SDTG	–	Social Development Thematic Group, Sustainable Development and Climate Change Department, ADB
SPRA	–	Results Management and Aid Effectiveness Division, Strategy, Policy, and Partnerships Department, ADB
STGs	–	sector and thematic groups
TA	–	technical assistance
UN	–	United Nations
UNICEF	–	United Nations Children's Fund
WBG	–	World Bank Group
WHO	–	World Health Organization

1 Rationale for Investing in Disability-Inclusive Development in the Asia and Pacific Region

Introduction

The Asia and Pacific region is home to around 70% of the global population of people with disabilities, or around 690 million people. In many countries in the region, more than half of all persons with disabilities are over 60 years old. Around 350 million women and girls in Asia and the Pacific live with disabilities (ESCAP 2017).[1] They often face various forms of discrimination based on gender and disability (Ortoleva and Lewis 2012).

People with disabilities in the region are among the poorest. They lack access to education, social protection, health and social care services, and employment and livelihood opportunities, and face barriers in the built environment, transport, and communications, and in access to information and assistive technology.

Poverty and disability are interrelated. Poor people are more likely to become disabled because of the conditions in which they live (GSDRC 2015); disability is likely to make people poorer because of discrimination and inequality of access to education, health and social protection services, employment, the built environment, transport, and information and communication facilities (ESCAP 2018b).

Compared with men without disabilities, women with disabilities are three times more likely to be illiterate, two times less likely to use the internet, three times more likely to have unmet health care needs, and two times less likely to be employed. Women and girls with disabilities who are migrants, refugees, or members of ethnic minorities experience even greater hardship and inequity (UN DESA 2020).

People with disabilities are doubly disadvantaged by the impact of climate change, with their well-being likely to be particularly affected in relation to food security, shelter, displacement, security, and access to water, sanitation, and hygiene (CBM, n.d.[a]). The added costs of disability can cause significant inequities, and social protection programs that take these costs into account are better able to lift people with disabilities out of poverty (OHCHR 2020).

By 2050, one in four people in Asia and the Pacific will be over 60 years old, and the number of people living with disabilities will have significantly increased. The population of older persons (aged over 60) in the region is projected to triple between 2010 and 2050, reaching close to 1.3 billion people by the end of the period (UNFPA Asia-Pacific Regional Office, n.d.). In some countries, such as the People's Republic of China (PRC), Sri Lanka, Thailand, and Viet Nam, this demographic shift will happen very rapidly; in others, such as Indonesia, the change will not be as quick, but these countries will still end up with very large populations of older persons. Disabilities arising from noncommunicable diseases are also becoming more prevalent

---

[1] These estimates are based on the WHO World Disability report (2011) finding that 15% of the global population lives with some form of disability and about one-fifth of this group have disabilities that are significant (ESCAP 2018).

worldwide, and particularly in the Pacific.[2] As a result, Asia and the Pacific, in the next few decades, could well have a population that is among the world's oldest and therefore have a larger percentage of people with disabilities than populations in other parts of the world.

This demographic transition will have wide-reaching social and economic consequences, for which governments in the region are generally poorly prepared. Social protection coverage in the region is low: only 28%–30% of persons with disabilities benefit from social protection measures like government-funded health care (ESCAP 2018b) and only 21.6% of people with severe disabilities are covered by disability benefits (ILO, n.d.).

It is important to adapt now to the expected change and prepare for a future where people with disabilities make up a larger share of the region's population.

The coronavirus disease has disproportionately affected people with disabilities and underscored their greater vulnerability to infection, serious illness, and death than other people. People with disabilities are more likely than other people to have poor access to support services—in health, social protection, or employment—and more likely to be excluded from education during the pandemic (Inclusive Futures 2020). Gender, disability, and structural inequalities, which typified societies before the crisis, are worsening because of the coronavirus disease (COVID-19) crisis. But the lack of gender- and disability-disaggregated data hampers evidence-based analysis of the socioeconomic impact of the pandemic, as well as policy targeting and mainstreaming (ESCAP 2017).

Disability-inclusive COVID-19 response and recovery requires the meaningful participation of people with diverse disabilities, through partnerships and consultation; continued access to services and public information; income security; safeguards for those living in social care facilities; and equitable access to health services and vaccines, especially for those most at risk and hardest to reach (ESCAP 2020). A disability-inclusive approach will be critical to ensuring that structural inequalities experienced by people with disabilities can be addressed. Adopting such an approach will enable countries to "build back better" according to their commitments under the Sendai Framework for Disaster Risk Reduction.[3] They will also be better able to reduce the factors underlying the disproportionate risk of extreme poverty and lack of access to health, education, employment, social protection, and other social services among people with disabilities and other excluded groups.

Failure to act has high economic costs, in addition to the human cost of exclusion. In low- and middle-income countries, a loss of 3%–7% of gross domestic product (GDP) resulting from the exclusion of people with disabilities from the labor market is estimated (Buckup 2009). Underemployment and unemployment of people with disabilities heightens economic and social exclusion.

Inclusive employment practices, reasonable accommodation, the use of digital assistive technologies, and the rise in new forms of work, especially the shift to online work, present opportunities to change employment paradigms for people with disabilities, and can help increase the proportion of people with disabilities in the workforce, improve economic inclusion, and raise GDP.

Addressing disability inclusion can and will make a difference for individuals, for communities, and for countries. Opportunities exist across all sectors to promote disability inclusion and thereby address the vulnerabilities of one of the important remaining "left-behind" groups, which are drivers of poverty and inequality in the region.

---

[2]   For example, diabetes-related amputations and blindness. Diabetes rates in some countries (e.g., Fiji, Samoa, Tonga) far exceed the 10% global prevalence rate (UNDP 2014, 86–90).

[3]   The Sendai Framework for Disaster Risk Reduction 2015–2030 (UNDRR 2015) outlines seven targets and four priorities for action to prevent new, and reduce existing, disaster risks: (i) understanding disaster risk; (ii) strengthening disaster risk governance to manage disaster risk; (iii) investing in disaster risk reduction for increased resilience; (iv) enhancing disaster preparedness for a more effective response; and (v) improved ability to "build back better."

International and Regional Agenda for Disability-Inclusive Development

To meet these challenges, countries must bring people with disabilities into the social mainstream so they can participate in daily life in their communities and contribute to socioeconomic development. International and regional agendas for disability-inclusive development provide strong foundations to build on.

The United Nations Convention on the Rights of Persons with Disabilities introduced a paradigm shift in the understanding of disability, from a welfare or medical model toward a model based on the rights of people with disabilities.[4] The United Nations Convention on the Rights of Persons with Disabilities (CRPD) has been ratified by 184 countries (United Nations 2021) since 2006, when it was first adopted by the UN.[5] The convention guarantees a range of political, civil, social, economic, and cultural rights, and social inclusion and equal opportunities for people with disabilities, as well as their full participation in the economic and social life of their communities.

Article 1 of the convention describes disabilities as "physical, mental, intellectual or sensory impairments which in interaction with various barriers may hinder [persons with disabilities from] full and effective participation in society on an equal basis with others."

Article 32 obligates governments to ensure that all persons with disabilities are part of their international cooperation programs, including their international development endeavors, and have ready access to those programs. Disability-inclusive development draws on this international disability rights framework and makes explicit the participation of people with disabilities in development programs (CBM, n.d.[b]).

Regular reports to the CRPD Committee by governments and organizations of persons with disabilities (OPDs) provide country-level monitoring and data on progress toward CRPD implementation. Concluding remarks by the CRPD Committee highlight gaps and ongoing challenges in implementation that governments must address.[6]

Global and regional development priorities are focused on achieving the Sustainable Development Goals by 2030. The Sustainable Development Goals (SDGs) issue a call to "leave no one behind" and refer to people with disabilities in various targets across the goals.[7] The goals require the disaggregation of key disability indicators so that existing inequities can be revealed and actions triggered to address them. Disability-inclusive development is recognized by all major multilateral and bilateral development banks, donor organizations, and other development actors as integral to fulfilling the SDG agenda to "leave no one behind" and to eradicate extreme poverty (see Box 1).

---

[4]   The four main models of disability are: the charity model, the medical model, the social model, and the human rights model. The first three focus on the source of the problem; the last, on finding solutions and creating an enabling environment for all (see CBM 2017, 20–23, for more information about these models of disability).

[5]   The Convention has been ratified by all ADB developing member countries except Bhutan, Solomon Islands, Tajikistan, and Tonga (which have signed, but not ratified, the agreement); and Niue and Timor-Leste (which have neither signed nor ratified the agreement).

[6]   CRPD Committee (2021) offers access to Committee reports and concluding remarks.

[7]   The SDGs are universal and apply to all people equally. People with disabilities are explicitly mentioned 11 times in the 2030 Agenda for Sustainable Development and especially in relation to SDG goals 4 on education; 8 on employment; 10 on economic, social, and political inclusion; and 11 on accessible cities, water, and transport, as well as 17 on data and monitoring. See, for example, United Nations (n.d.).

> ### Box 1: Disability-Inclusive Development, as Defined by a Range of Development Organizations[a]
>
> - The goal of **ending extreme poverty cannot be achieved without disability-inclusive development.**
>
> - Disability-inclusive development recognizes and is responsive to the **intersection of disability with other drivers of discrimination,** such as gender, ethnicity, religion, age, and national or social origin, that can compound exclusion and disadvantage.
>
> - **Disability-inclusive development explicitly includes people with disabilities** in development processes as participants and as beneficiaries.
>
> - Disability-inclusive development is facilitated and implemented in **multilateral and multisectoral partnerships** with governments, development banks, the private sector, and civil society **to raise awareness and leverage impact.**
>
> - Disability inclusion can be mainstreamed across institutions and implemented in targeted programs and projects. Adopting both approaches is known as a twin-track approach.
>
> - Disability-inclusive development is based on a **multisectoral life-cycle approach** including the following elements and focus areas: early childhood development, inclusive education, community-based development, supported independent living, employment, livelihoods and economic empowerment, active aging, inclusive social protection, available and affordable health services and assistive technology, accessibility (of transport, urban environment, information and communication technology, water, social services), inclusive emergency preparedness and response, and improved data and information about people with disabilities.[b]
>
> ---
>
> [a] See also Appendix 2 for an overview of different donor approaches and strategies for disability inclusive development.
> [b] Some development institutions also include the prevention of impairments (e.g., by investing in road safety programs) within the scope of disability-inclusive development, while others explicitly do not (DFAT 2015, 9). Some emphasize the inclusion in disability-inclusive development of people who are often excluded from disability data and programming, such as older people, people with "invisible" disabilities, or people with mental health conditions.
> Sources: DFID (now FCDO), DFAT, World Bank.

In 2012, governments in the region declared 2013–2022 the third Asian and Pacific "Decade of Persons with Disabilities." Building on the CPRD, they adopted the Incheon Strategy to "Make the Right Real" for Persons with Disabilities in Asia and the Pacific (ESCAP 2012) to track progress toward improving the quality of life and the fulfillment of the rights of the 690 million persons with disabilities in the region, most of whom live in poverty. This strategy provides Asia and the Pacific with its first set of regionally agreed disability-inclusive development goals—10 goals, with 27 targets and 62 indicators.

The Incheon Strategy's target and indicator framework calls for improvements in the reliability and comparability of disability data, and for the United Nations Economic and Social Commission on Asia and the Pacific (ESCAP) members and associate members to report on disability-specific indicators that measure progress toward disability-inclusive development in the region. The ESCAP secretariat is mandated to report every 3 years until the end of the Asian and Pacific Decade in 2022, on progress in the implementation of the ministerial declaration and the Incheon Strategy.

In 2017, governments in the region adopted the Beijing Declaration, including the Action Plan to Accelerate the Implementation of the Incheon Strategy. Progress in implementing the strategy had been slow across all areas of the CRPD by the midpoint of the Asian and Pacific Decade of Persons with Disabilities, 2013–2022, and monitoring was constrained especially by the lack of reliable data on people with disabilities

(ESCAP 2018a). For each goal of the Incheon Strategy, the Beijing Declaration and Action Plan provides recommendations for strategic policy measures to accelerate implementation that can be taken by governments and civil society stakeholders. It also focuses on operational synergy between the Incheon Strategy and the 2030 Agenda for Sustainable Development, reaffirms member states' commitment to accelerate the implementation of the Incheon Strategy, revisits persistent challenges faced by persons with disabilities, and highlights major actions to be taken by ESCAP in the remaining years of implementation (ESCAP 2019b).

Disability is an important component of overall diversity, and development organizations across the world have been adopting policies and frameworks to support disability inclusion within their institutions. Organizations committed to disability-inclusive development are more credible and effective if they themselves are committed to disability diversity in their workplace and internal policies and practices. Independent studies have shown "a strong correlation between workplace inclusion of employees with disabilities and increased productivity, reduced absenteeism, reduced turnover, increased morale, more positive organizational culture and reduced workers' compensation."[8]

Some organizations, such as the World Bank Group (WBG), the Department of Foreign Affairs and Trade (DFAT) of Australia, and the Foreign, Commonwealth & Development Office (FCDO) of the United Kingdom, are moving toward disability inclusion in their workplaces. The WBG committed at the Global Disability Summit in 2018 to employing more people with disabilities. In 2019, it reported that it was taking steps to fulfill this commitment by drafting a disability directive and by creating a new human resource information system to record data about staff who want to identify as persons with disabilities. DFAT has been pursuing a disability-inclusive employment strategy since 2015 (see Appendix 2). In 2018, the FCDO introduced disability inclusion standards in all of its offices (DFID 2018c; FCDO 2020), and the United Nations launched its Disability Inclusion Strategy in 2019 (United Nations 2019).

The implementation of the CRPD, the Incheon Strategy and the Beijing Action Plan, and the SDGs, and the emerging focus on and commitment to these issues within the international development agencies, represent a strong foundation for taking a disability-inclusive development approach in the Asia and Pacific region and in the Asian Development Bank (ADB).

Challenges in Measuring the Prevalence of Disability and Understanding the Situation of People with Disabilities

Having good data on people with disabilities is essential to understanding disability prevalence and deciding on approaches to disability inclusion. Administrative data are among the main sources of information about people with disabilities, including the following: number of recipients of disability allowances or other benefits; number of people using social and rehabilitation services; medical data on the number of people with certain medical diagnoses; and education sector data on the number of children and young people with special educational needs in schools or higher education institutions.

However, administrative data sets are often contradictory and incomplete, as disability may not be consistently defined across sectors and ministries, administrative data are often not disaggregated by disability status, and management information systems may not be interoperable across government entities.

---

[8]   See, for example, Australian Network on Disability (n.d.) and Diversity Council Australia (n.d.); cited in DFAT (2016)

Census tallies and other national surveys are important sources of data, but disability prevalence rates can vary depending on the questions asked, rather than on any common or "given" definition of disability. For example, asking the question "Do you have a disability?" may provoke stigma among people who identify as disabled. Also, disability implies a significant condition but is often interpreted in relation to a perceived norm, so people who consider their disability less severe may not be included. An older person having difficulty in performing basic activities but thinking he or she is performing as well as can be expected for a person of that age may not identify as disabled (Mont 2007).

Other data challenges can arise from evolving understanding and definition of disability, as well as from the lack of statistical capacity in governments for collecting, processing, disaggregating, and analyzing data.

In response to these challenges, the Washington Group on Disability Statistics was established in 2001 to create standardized indicators of disability (Washington Group on Disability Statistics, n.d.). It drew up a set of questions based on functional limitations, simple enough to be used in census data collection and other surveys but providing valid comparative estimates of disability across countries (see Box 2).[9] This set of questions was recommended by the UN Statistical Commission and the UN Economic Commission for Europe's Conference of European Statisticians for the 2020 round of censuses, and has been endorsed for disability data segregation for the SDGs by the Disability Data Expert Group under the UN Department of Economic and Social Affairs.

The United Nations Children's Fund (UNICEF) and the Washington Group have also adapted these questions for use in surveys of children aged 2–17 years (Washington Group on Disability Statistics 2016). In addition, the International Labour Organization and the Washington Group have recently developed the Labor Force Survey Disability Module to facilitate the collection of employment data.

The World Health Organization (WHO) has developed a disability assessment schedule, WHO-DAS 2 (WHO 2021b), a tool for producing standardized disability levels and profiles that can be used across cultures and in all

---

Box 2: Washington Group Questions
(Short Set)

- Do you have difficulty **seeing**, even if wearing glasses?

- Do you have difficulty **hearing**, even if using a hearing aid?

- Do you have difficulty **walking or climbing** steps?

- Do you have difficulty **remembering or concentrating**?

- Do you have difficulty with (**self-care** such as) washing all over or dressing?

- Using your usual (customary) language, do you have difficulty **communicating**, for example, understanding or being understood?

Four categories of answers are used: a. No difficulty; b. Some difficulty; c. A lot of difficulty; d. Cannot do at all.

The Washington Group recommends using categories "c" and "d" for "people with disabilities," and also "b" if the intention is to widen access to services or to disaster response and recovery programs.

Source: Washington Group on Disability Statistics (2016).

---

[9]   ADB used these questions in household surveys in a study of social services linked with social assistance in the PRC (under a technical assistance project) and a review of the situation of people with disabilities in Mongolia (under a project preparatory technical assistance project).

adult populations, and is directly linked conceptually to the International Classification of Functioning, Disability and Health. There is a short (5-minute) version as well as a longer (20-minute) version, in both clinical and general study settings.

Using these questions in project surveys can help in identifying people with different types of functional limitations and in better capturing their experience and analyzing their situation. Designing research that can engage with people with diverse disabilities and ensure their participation is also important in achieving disability-inclusive development.

Poverty Reduction and Disability-Inclusive Development

There is evidence of a strong link between disability and poverty (CBM 2016). According to the results of a systematic review of disability and poverty published in 2014 by the International Centre for Evidence in Disability at the London School of Hygiene & Tropical Medicine, the inclusion of people with disabilities in employment can increase economic independence through better employment opportunities and more inclusive work environments (Morgon Banks and Pollack 2014, 35–46; cited in DFID 2018a). Persons with disabilities are two to six times more likely to be unemployed than those without disabilities.

Promoting the inclusion of children with disabilities in education can also generate economic development. Studies have found that in the PRC, every extra year of school completed by children with disabilities led to a 5%–8% increase in their wages as adults. In the Philippines and Nepal, education has an even greater impact on wages, which have been shown to increase by more than 20% for each additional year of education that children with disabilities complete.[10]

Government social protection programs often have limited coverage of people with disabilities. In some countries in the Asia and Pacific region, only 28%–30% of persons with disabilities benefit from social protection measures such as government-funded health care and disability benefits, and persons with disabilities are 3.9%–20.6% poorer than the overall population (ESCAP 2018b). Development organizations and governments worldwide increasingly recognize that reducing poverty, especially chronic poverty among particularly disadvantaged and vulnerable population groups, requires taking a disability-inclusive development approach.

Multiple and Intersectional Vulnerability: Women and Girls with Disabilities

In most areas of life, women and girls face many barriers resulting from the interplay between poverty and gender- and disability-based discrimination, which hinder access to equal opportunities for education, employment, and social interaction (CRPD Committee 2015). Vulnerability to violence also increases significantly, especially among women with intellectual disabilities (DFAT 2015).

General Comment No. 3 of the CRPD Committee emphasizes the various vulnerabilities of women and girls with disabilities and the need to be attentive to their inclusion and active participation: "It is not enough to take

---

[10]   Studies from the PRC; Hong Kong, China; and the Philippines, cited in CBM (2016, 60).

women with disabilities into account when designing development measures; rather, women with disabilities must also be able to participate in and contribute to society" (CRPD Committee 2015).

Studies show that women with disabilities in low- to middle-income countries are twice to four times as likely to experience intimate partner violence than other women (Dunkle et al. 2018). DFAT research has found that women with disabilities in the Asia and Pacific region are not only more likely to experience violence than women without disabilities but are also victims of different kinds of violence, such as withholding of medication and forced sterilization (Spratt 2013, 12; cited in DFAT 2015). Further DFAT research findings highlight the disproportionate family violence experienced by women and girls with disabilities and their lack of access to appropriate support services as a result of discrimination (Astbury and Walji 2013; cited in DFAT 2015).

There are reports that women have suffered more intimate partner violence during the COVID-19 pandemic and it is likely that women with disabilities have been disproportionately affected (OCHA 2020). ADB's COVID-19 response programs have had a strong focus on domestic and intimate partner violence, but there is a need to ensure that the intersection of gender and disability is adequately considered.

Women and girls are commonly the primary caregivers for household members with disabilities, and this role limits their opportunities for education and employment and can affect their physical and mental health, especially when they are required to provide high levels of care (DFAT 2015).

Older People and Disability

Disabilities become more likely to occur and more prevalent with increasing age. More than 46% of older persons over the age of 60 years live with disabilities, and older persons make up the majority of the overall population of persons with disabilities. With the number of older people in Asia and the Pacific increasing rapidly, life expectancy getting longer, and exposure to risks of noncommunicable diseases and dementia increasing, the number of persons living with disability in the region is expected to rise (ESCAP 2019a).

Older persons with disability face exclusion and multiple layers of discrimination based on their disability and their age, such as increased risks of deprivation of legal capacity and institutionalization. In many countries where disability programs do exist, these explicitly exclude older persons who acquire a disability late in life (United Nations General Assembly 2019).

Often, many older people who acquire disabilities in later life do not self-identify as disabled because of the stigma and expectations around the aging process. Disability-inclusive development can have an impact on economic engagement, inclusion, expansion of social protection, lifelong learning, accessible health and care services, and quality of life of older people with disabilities (Box 3).

Challenges in the collection and reporting of disability data are compounded when older people are involved. Household surveys, such as the demographic and health surveys (DHSs), which are important sources of data in low- and middle-income countries, do not gather data on household members over 59 years of age (HelpAge International and AARP 2018). A mapping of aging-related statistics in the Asia and Pacific region has shown that the majority of countries collect information about disability, but with a lack of consistency in the types of disability covered. Some countries ask about five types of impairment—mobility, vision, hearing, speech, and cognition—while others include only two or three types (DFID 2018c; FCDO 2020), and some stop counting disabled people when they qualify for old age pensions (ADB 2019a).

Box 3: A Perfect Storm of Exclusion and Marginalization—The Intersection of Disability with Aging, Gender, and Extreme Poverty

Given the dynamics and intersections of disability prevalence, demographic transition, gender, and poverty, the Asia and Pacific region will face many challenges and new forms of exclusion and marginalization in the coming years. Developing effective approaches to addressing the current and emerging needs should be priorities for all.

- Persons 60 and over in the Asia and Pacific region are projected to increase rapidly, from 12% of the population in the region in 2017 to 24% by 2050.

- Globally, 54% of persons aged 60 and over are women.

- More than 46% of older persons—those aged 60 years and over—have disabilities.

- Income insecurity is the norm: only 1 in 4 older persons receives a pension.

- Women have longer life expectancy than men and live a greater proportion of their lives in poorer health, resulting in higher rates of disability in older women, heightened by vulnerabilities accumulated across the life course including lack of access to education, pensions, inheritance, and paid work.

Sources: HelpAge International (2015); HelpAge International and AARP (2018); UN DESA/Population Division (2017).

2 Disability Inclusion Is Essential to the Effective Implementation of Strategy 2030

The Asia and Pacific region faces considerable challenges in relation to disability exclusion, inequality, and extreme poverty, both as the home to a significant proportion of the world's people with disabilities and as a rapidly aging region. Governments in the region have demonstrated leadership in implementing the CRPD, through the Incheon Strategy and the Beijing Action Plan, among other goal-setting frameworks and courses of action. But people with disabilities in the region continue to be affected by social exclusion and nonfulfillment of their rights (ESCAP 2018b), and the COVID-19 crisis has exposed and worsened this exclusion (Alisjahbana 2020; Uji and Bjorkman 2021).

Constraints on inclusion in education persist throughout life, especially for children and adults with intellectual disabilities (ESCAP 2018b; UNESCO 2018; UNICEF EAPRO 2020). People with disabilities do not have equitable access to health care across the region (ESCAP 2018b), and health services that address disability, such as habilitation and rehabilitation services or mental health services, are considerably under-provided in many countries (WHO 2021a). People with disabilities continue to be underemployed or unemployed, and their poor access to the built environment and to transportation, information, and communication facilities, despite some improvements, continues to hamper their economic and social participation (ESCAP 2018b).

ADB's Strategy 2030 commits ADB to increasing its emphasis on social inclusion and human development to address the non-income dimensions of poverty. The strategy's first operational priority is addressing remaining poverty and reducing inequalities through a three-pronged strategy: investing in human capital and social protection, facilitating access to good-quality jobs, and reducing inequality of opportunity through such means as removing barriers to access to infrastructure and services, especially for the poor and vulnerable.

ADB is committed to directing its concessional financing to support its poorest and most vulnerable members (including persons with disabilities) and to considering additional support for countries graduating from concessional assistance. The importance of disability inclusion is also included in several other operational priorities—notably OP 2 (Accelerating Progress in Gender Equality) and OP4 (Making Cities More Livable).

ADB has developed tools and experience to support disability inclusion. The inclusive and sustainable growth assessments under its country partnership strategies (CPSs) and the poverty and social assessments done in projects are mandatory components of due diligence and documentation at the country and project level.

In 2005, ADB published a disability brief, which gave an overview of the key issues and outlined tools for addressing the needs of people with disabilities and integrating those needs into poverty and social assessments and project design (ADB 2005). The 2012 Handbook on Poverty and Social Assessment provides guidance on consultation and on risk and opportunity assessment for vulnerable groups, including persons with disabilities (ADB 2012).

In 2014, ADB published a Guidance Note on Poverty and Social Dimensions in Urban Projects (ADB 2014), and in 2016, it published a Tool Kit for Inclusive Urban Development (ADB 2016); both publications address the consideration of socially excluded people, including people with disabilities. The Guidance Note on COVID-19 and Livable Cities in Asia and the Pacific (ADB 2020a), published by ADB in 2021, provides guidance on enhancing inclusivity through greater social protection measures for vulnerable groups in cities, including people with disabilities.

ADB can build on this experience in current projects involving disability-inclusive development. ADB is supporting inclusive education for children and youth with disabilities in Bangladesh, Mongolia, and Viet Nam, and has several disability-inclusive transport and infrastructure projects, such as the Mumbai Metro project, which actively target people with disabilities and get them involved in monitoring implementation. (Many other infrastructure projects are also helping to remove barriers in the built environment for people with disabilities but do not explicitly target people with disabilities and therefore cannot be classified as disability inclusive; see Appendix 3 for a summary of ADB's disability inclusion indicator and methodology.)

In Mongolia, ADB approved a disability-targeted loan and technical assistance (TA) projects involving inclusion and services for people with disabilities in 2017, and inclusive education in 2020. In Georgia and Pakistan, the ADB-assisted urban and transport programs have both been influential in developing guidance on inclusive design.

ADB has also joined in international efforts to support disability inclusion and to raise awareness of the issue. ADB took part in the first Global Disability Summit in 2018, hosted by the Department for International Development (DFID) of the United Kingdom, the International Disability Alliance, and the Government of Kenya, and signed the Charter for Change, which seeks to deliver on the CRPD commitments and the SDGs for persons with disabilities (DFID, Government of Kenya, and IDA 2018). Along with other multilateral development banks and international institutions, ADB committed itself to supporting disability inclusion across nine areas of investment and research (see Box 4).

Box 4: ADB's Global Disability Summit Commitments

- Undertake an assessment and develop a strategic road map for disability inclusion in the Asian Development Bank (ADB) to support its new corporate Strategy 2030 and to develop capacity within ADB.

- Engage in coordinated advocacy of disability inclusion via membership in the Global Action on Disability Network.

- Participate actively in intergovernmental meetings related to the implementation of the Incheon Strategy.

- Review the existing education portfolio, to identify gaps and the potential for supporting more effectively the social inclusion of the most marginalized children, such as out-of-school girls and boys with disabilities.

- Support innovations to expand the quality, scope, and range of accessible materials and teaching approaches for learners with disabilities, and make their physical environment more accessible via universal design.

- Invest in accessible vocational training programs for people with disabilities, and in capacity-building programs for training institutions, both government and private.

- Conduct research into developing inclusive insurance markets to make available risk management products that cover low-income households in case of death or serious disability.

- Analyze data on social protection coverage for persons with disabilities in the Asia and Pacific region, from ADB's social protection indicator database.

- Incorporate disability inclusion in universal health coverage strategies and reforms and in the design of hospitals and health facilities for the future.

continued on next page

Box 4 *continued*

The time frame for these commitments began in mid-2018. The Foreign, Commonwealth & Development Office (FCDO) of the United Kingdom and the International Disability Alliance are coordinating regular reporting on progress in delivering on these commitments, as part of commitment 10 (to "be and hold others accountable") under the Charter for Change of 2018. ADB is making progress toward fulfilling these commitments, which this road map is expected to further strengthen and expand.

Source: Authors, lifting the list of commitments from International Disability Alliance. All Commitments made by Asian Development Bank. https://www.internationaldisabilityalliance.org/commitments/stakeholder/asian-development-bank.

Since 2015, ADB has also been a member of the Global Action on Disability (GLAD) Network, a coordinating body of bilateral and multilateral donors and agencies, the private sector, and foundations working to improve the inclusion of persons with disabilities in international development and humanitarian action. ADB collaboration with the GLAD Network on knowledge sharing and events is ongoing.

In 2019, during the development of the Strategy 2030 Corporate Results Framework, it was agreed that reporting on poverty and inequality should be strengthened and that an indicator should be developed to measure disability inclusion. ADB has accordingly developed a disability inclusion indicator and is currently pilot-testing a marker system for measuring the indicator. The first report on disability inclusion in the 2019 Development Effectiveness Review stated that "the share of operations committed in 2019 considered disability-inclusive or creating enabling conditions for disability inclusion was 22%" (ADB 2020b).

Guidance on applying the marker in projects is being drafted and pilot-tested in 2020–2021 under the leadership of the Social Development Thematic Group (SDTG) of the Sustainable Development and Climate Change Department, and the Results Management and Aid Effectiveness Division (SPRA) of the Strategy, Policy, and Partnerships Department. (A brief overview of the indicator and the first results of the pilot testing of the draft methodology for the marker system can be found in Appendix 3.)

Within ADB, the goal is to build a truly diverse and inclusive workplace, where all employees feel they belong and can achieve their full potential. Employees who feel a strong sense of belonging at work are more likely to bring their best selves to work and do their best work.

In 2021, ADB is therefore developing a new Diversity, Inclusion, and Belonging (DIB) Framework to foster a culture of diversity, belonging, and inclusion within the organization. The DIB Framework will outline goals that will serve as the foundation for workplace inclusion and will help guide future action in new areas, including disability inclusion. It will show how ADB will work toward becoming an even more inclusive employer and build an even more inclusive organizational culture for all, including people with disabilities.

A first step toward addressing the needs of people with disabilities will be conducting a gap analysis to benchmark ADB's practices and culture against best practices followed worldwide and by other international development finance institutions. ADB can thus build a future road map of tangible actions to support sustainable disability inclusion by identifying areas where progress can be accelerated and have the greatest impact. A gap analysis is expected to help ADB set goals around key human resource policies and practices in areas like recruitment and employment practices, reasonable accommodation, and employee reporting, besides strengthening the organizational culture to reduce stigma and stereotyping. The analysis can also suggest other areas where inclusion support can be provided, such as workplace facilities and accessibility, institutional and operational procurement, and communications.

ADB is well positioned to build on its track record and regional leadership role, and on its strengths as an investor in social development and infrastructure, to create and gradually implement a coherent dual-track, disability-inclusive development framework and actions to support the implementation of its Strategy 2030. At the same time, ADB can move toward mainstreaming disability inclusion in its own workplace and into its business practices and policies. This road map is a first step in these processes.

3 ADB Opportunities, Options, and Challenges in Disability-Inclusive Development in the Context of Strategy 2030

ADB's available tools, interventions, and learning from the experiences of bilateral donors and other international organizations provide the basis for strengthening disability-inclusive development further, in line with Strategy 2030, the Incheon Strategy and the Beijing Action Plan, the CRPD, and the SDG agenda. Recognition of the need for increased efforts to promote disability-inclusive development is growing worldwide and in the region.

How best to integrate a disability-inclusive approach across the different sectors and themes and across the different regional departments is a continuing internal challenge. At the same time, country programming and the various stages of project preparation—conceptualization, project planning, and detailed design—offer opportunities for people with disabilities to participate in projects and derive benefits from them. Strong mechanisms for cross-sector and cross-thematic information sharing and capacity building will have to be developed.

External challenges include the lack of valid disaggregated data on people with disabilities, and of common definitions and methods for conducting research and surveys on people with disabilities. The questions developed by the Washington Group on Disability Statistics for identifying people with disabilities and for including and reporting disability data from research and surveys (see Box 2) are being used by many agencies and governments to address these challenges. But consistent application is required to build up disaggregated data to support SDG monitoring and to form the basis for disability-inclusive development (Washington Group on Disability Statistics, n.d.). See Box 5 for an analysis of ADB's readiness to support disability-inclusive development.

Moving toward Disability-Inclusive Development

Developing more effective approaches to disability inclusion requires a strategic road map for action. The road map—its development was the first commitment made by ADB during the 2018 Global Disability Summit—provides a framework for moving toward disability-inclusive development that can be used both internally by staff and externally by partners or collaborators and developing member countries (DMCs).

In the short and medium term, ADB will work to achieve quick wins that build on its considerable experience in gender mainstreaming and social inclusion, and on its role as a leader in the Asia and Pacific region in knowledge and resources related to infrastructure, education, health, social protection, and other areas affecting people with disabilities. These efforts will involve integrating disability inclusion into program and project planning,

Box 5: SWOT Analysis of ADB's Readiness to Support Disability-Inclusive Development

	Helpful In Achieving the Objective	Harmful To Achieving the Objective
Internal Organization	**Strengths** • Inclusive and sustainable growth assessment at the country level • Poverty and social assessment at the project level • Disability Brief • Road map for inclusive development • Committed support for disability inclusion in S2030, in several OPs • Disability inclusion indicator (part of the corporate results framework since 2019) and process of finalizing methodology • Diversity, Inclusion, and Belonging Framework being developed in 2021	**Weaknesses** • Lack of internal specialized capacity for disability inclusion, and dedicated funding to support pilot testing and innovation in disability-inclusive development • Lack of awareness of issues and options to support disability-inclusive development through research and project portfolio • Constraints on incorporating meaningful engagement with OPDs into business processes and the project cycle
External Environment	**Opportunities** • Adoption of the Incheon Strategy and the Beijing Action Plan by countries in the Asia and Pacific region, confirming their commitment to CRPD ratification and implementation • Recognition of disability-inclusive development as integral to fulfilling the SDG agenda by 2030	**Challenges** • Projected increase in number of persons with disability due to rapid population aging in the region • Lack of data • Lack of DMC awareness and willingness to prioritize disability-inclusive development in engagement with ADB

ADB = Asian Development Bank; CRPD = United Nations Convention on the Rights of Persons with Disabilities; DMC = developing member country; OP = Operational Priority; OPD = organization of persons with disabilities; SDG = Sustainable Development Goal; S2030 = Strategy 2030; SWOT = strengths, weaknesses, opportunities, and threats.

implementation, and monitoring, as well as gradually building the capacity to work with DMCs in planning and implementing disability-targeted projects (ADB, forthcoming).[11]

Recognizing the wealth of knowledge of disability inclusion among international and national nongovernment organizations (NGOs) and their experience in this matter, ADB will engage with organizations of persons with disabilities (OPDs) and civil society organizations (CSOs) experienced in disability inclusion, both through a reference group and in national and regional operations.

Effectively, this road map sets a course across five core components for moving toward full mainstreaming of disability inclusion (as defined in HelpAge International and AARP 2018) in the long term. It also focuses on short- to medium-term actions in ADB project and program planning, strategic procurement planning,

---

[11]   *Disability-targeted projects* are designed with disabled persons as target beneficiaries. The project may stand alone or be a subcomponent of a larger program. This ensures that people with disabilities are explicitly provided with the same access as others to basic and essential services, and to infrastructure. Disability mainstreaming creates an institution-wide commitment to addressing disability inclusion in all activities, and in all human resource and procurement policies.

implementation, and monitoring, as ADB addresses the issue mainly through disability-targeted interventions and knowledge development, strives for greater inclusion in its employment practices, and generally promotes an organizational culture that is even more inclusive.

Implementing Disability-Inclusive Development across ADB: Five Core Components

Component 1: Coordinate actions related to disability inclusion across the different ADB departments and sectors, and develop the capacity for disability-inclusive development within the organization. This component is a prerequisite for all other actions. Building a common understanding of disability, inclusion, and participation among the staff will support mainstreaming across organizational silos. It will also ensure that ADB staff can interact effectively with government and other counterparts for the gradual strengthening of disability-inclusive development within ADB portfolios and operations.

Developing a common understanding among staff of disability-inclusive development across sectors and themes, consistent with the CRPD, SDG, and Incheon Strategy and Beijing Action Plan policy frameworks, and enabling their reliable use of the ADB disability marker in assessing the extent of disability inclusion in their programs, will build confidence in ADB as a credible disability-inclusive development agency and support the implementation of the four other components.

Figure 1: Road Map for Implementing Disability-Inclusive Development Core Components

COMPONENT 1: Coordinate actions on disability inclusion across different departments and sectors of ADB and develop capacity within the organization.

COMPONENT 2: Establish partnerships to leverage advocacy impact.

COMPONENT 3: Establish a culture of data disaggregation and publishing disability-sensitive analysis.

COMPONENT 4: Develop sector guidelines and gradually expand portfolio of disability-inclusive development interventions.

COMPONENT 5: Strengthen disability inclusion standards in ADB workplaces, policies, and practices.

Source: Author.

Component 2: Strategic partnerships to leverage impact. ADB, on its own, cannot achieve disability inclusion or its Strategy 2030 goals. Strategic partnerships with other actors in disability-inclusive development at the global, regional, subregional, and national levels, including OPDs, can speed up the implementation of Strategy 2030 priorities and magnify the impact of ADB investments in individual countries and at the regional level.

Partnerships established with CBM Australia, the Global Disability Innovation Hub (GDIH), and the GLAD Network are already facilitating the implementation of disability-inclusive development approaches at ADB. These partnerships can help to make up for the lack of dedicated disability inclusion specialists internally in the short term, and to identify how this capacity can best be developed or procured over the longer term.

A range of other regional and international organizations and networks are also important strategic partners in leveraging investment in disability inclusion or augmenting its impact. For example, UNICEF, the Inclusive Education Initiative, and the Global Partnership for Education are all important ADB partners in inclusive education. ESCAP is a key regional partner in CRPD implementation, especially in strengthening data systems to support disability-disaggregated data, and partnerships with both ESCAP and the International Labour Organization are of noteworthy value in promoting inclusive social protection and employment.

In addition, each thematic group and regional team in ADB can identify potential strategic partnerships with national, regional, subregional, and international OPDs and other groups that can create synergies to heighten impact across all aspects of disability-inclusive development.

Component 3: Establish a culture of data collection and disaggregation, and publication of disability-sensitive analyses. Institutionalizing the use of Washington Group questions and building the capacity of OPDs, research organizations, line ministries, and national statistics offices for data collection and disaggregation, where appropriate, will also help to strengthen projects and ensure the robust cross-organizational application of the disability inclusion indicator in corporate reporting.

ADB already has access to a range of data on people with disabilities that were gathered as part of project scoping and planning processes but have not yet been examined and analyzed through a disability lens. Mining existing data can generate new knowledge, contribute to capacity building internally and with partners, and provide a solid foundation for developing disability-inclusive programs and projects and mainstreaming disability inclusion into the different stages of the ADB project cycle. Collaborating with OPDs, with disability experts, and with people with disabilities themselves will validate the findings and highlight gaps where further research may be required.

ADB can also build on its experience in gender mainstreaming, gender-disaggregated data collection, and synergy building across thematic areas. An ongoing safeguard-strengthening initiative (ADB 2019c) is aimed at building an integrated safeguard monitoring system that will cover disability and other social issues and can be a source of disability inclusion data for ADB.

Component 4: Develop sector guidelines and gradually expand the portfolio of disability-inclusive development interventions. ADB and project staff interact regularly with governments and can gradually sensitize government partners to the economic and other advantages of adopting disability-inclusive programs and projects. Prioritizing universal and/or inclusive design (United Nations 2008),[12] encouraging people with disabilities among the project beneficiaries to take part in project planning and poverty and social assessments (including surveys and community consultations to identify safeguard issues), understanding their situation, and recognizing these project beneficiaries as fundamental to infrastructure projects can achieve quick wins across

---

[12] Article 2 of the Convention defines universal design as "the design of products, environments, programs and services to be usable by all people, to the greatest extent possible, without the need for adaptation or specialized design. Universal design shall not exclude assistive devices for particular groups of persons with disabilities where this is needed."

the transport, inclusive cities, and other sectors where building and construction are central to ADB projects (such as schools and hospitals). Project evaluations that consider how people with disabilities can be reached through accessible communication, have been included in projects, and are benefiting from them will manifest ADB's contributions and promote disability-inclusive development.

The needs of people with disabilities should be taken into account across all sectors—including finance; emergency response (such as COVID-19 response and recovery projects); climate resilience; and water, sanitation, and hygiene (WASH)—to help lay the foundations for disability inclusion in ADB operations. Funding modalities such as TA and grants can be used strategically to support the long-term development of a pipeline of disability-targeted projects or components.

The participation of OPDs and people with disabilities in CPSs, poverty and social analysis processes, and scoping studies and consultations associated with project preparation, implementation, and monitoring and evaluation will give ADB and its government partners a better understanding of the critical importance of disability-inclusive development in addressing Strategy 2030 priorities, the SDGs, the Incheon Strategy and the Beijing Action Plan, and CRPD implementation.

Component 5: Strengthen disability inclusion standards in the ADB workplace, and in its policies and practices. ADB plans to develop a Diversity, Inclusion, and Belonging Framework in 2021, under ADB's Budget, Personnel, and Management Systems Department (BPMSD) and Procurement, Portfolio, and Financial Management Department (PPFD) to provide a blueprint for future action, as well as a foundation for mainstreaming disability inclusion across ADB's employment and business practices. Gap analysis and benchmarking, to be done in 2022, would identify areas where ADB can proactively review and update policies and practices, including those related to institutional and operational procurement.

By implementing the DIB Framework, ADB can put in place, for example, ways to enable people with disabilities to voluntarily self-identify. Specific goals and timelines can be developed once the gap analysis is complete.

4 ADB Road Map for Disability-Inclusive Development Linked to Strategy 2030

This road map has the overall goal of developing a more systematic approach to implementing disability-inclusive development in ADB, starting in the period 2021–2025.[13] It focuses specifically on short- and medium-term actions, across the five core priority components, to introduce disability-inclusive development approaches and further build an inclusive organizational culture that can accelerate and strengthen the implementation of Strategy 2030 goals and priority areas.[14]

Disability-Inclusive Development Activities, 2021–2025

For each strategically linked disability-inclusive development and Strategy 2030 area, priority actions have been identified to build capacity, strengthen disability-inclusive program design, and enhance implementation within a 5-year period (2021–2025). Many of these actions will affect several areas linked with disability-inclusive development and Strategy 2030 but are organized here according to where they will have the most impact. Actions under the core components are also grouped here according to their impact on the achievement of Strategy 2030.

Component 1: Coordinate actions related to disability inclusion across ADB departments and sectors and develop capacity for disability-inclusive development within the organization

1.1 **Finalize this road map and develop guidance on disability-inclusive development** (2021; led by the Social Development Thematic Group [SDTG]). This road map will serve as internal guide over the short and medium term and set out ADB's intentions regarding the strengthening of disability inclusion, for an external audience.

1.2 **Update the 2005 Disability Brief** (2022; SDTG) and provide tools for integrating disability into country programming and projects, ensuring that poverty and social analysis guidance examines causes of social exclusion and encourages the participation of people with disabilities, as well as data disaggregation, in all stages of the project cycle. Including case studies of ADB project experience and operational engagement with DMCs in disability inclusion will also help in identifying areas where different approaches and nuances in national and regional contexts have had positive impact.

---

[13] This road map represents the first steps toward fulfilling ADB's Charter for Change commitment 1 from the Global Disability Summit, 2018.
[14] See Appendix 1 for a summary of the five components, key actions, and proposals for monitoring implementation.

1.3 **Develop guidance on the corporate disability inclusion indicator and marker system** (2019–2021; SDTG and the Results Management and Aid Effectiveness Division [SPRA] of the Strategy, Policy, and Partnerships Department). Pilot testing of the methodology was completed in 2020. After feedback from the departments is incorporated, the methodology guidance note will be finalized and disseminated to the departments.

1.4 **Identify and engage with a disability inclusion reference group** (2021–2025; SDTG, BPMSD) composed of national and regional OPDs and NGOs of parents of children with disabilities, as well as academics and experts in disability-inclusive development from member countries, well placed to inform, shape, and validate ADB's approach to strengthening disability-inclusive development across operations and to help ADB to stay updated and connected with relevant regional and global networks, initiatives, and resources. Group members will serve for 2–3 years.

The main purpose of this reference group is to support the implementation of the ADB road map for disability-inclusive development, and the participation of people with disabilities in informing, shaping, and monitoring disability-inclusive development in ADB operations. One of its tasks will be to review, strengthen, and endorse this road map and help ADB to chart the way forward (see the draft terms of reference for this reference group in Appendix 4).

1.5 **Build capacity for, and knowledge of, disability-inclusive development among ADB staff** (2021–2025; SDTG, sector and thematic groups [STGs], Knowledge Advisory Services Center, and BPMSD). A regular, sustained series of training and information events should be organized, TA provided, and materials published to raise awareness of disability-inclusive development among managers and staff across all sectors, thematic groups, and regional operations departments at ADB headquarters and in country offices, and gradually fill gaps in their understanding and knowledge of the issue. Understanding of how the pilot methodology for applying the disability inclusion marker is to be used in ADB projects and programs should be developed.

ADB staff and partners should gain technical knowledge of multidimensional and multisector disability-inclusive development approaches such as inclusive design, participatory planning, monitoring and implementation, and provision of reasonable accommodation (through assistive technology and other means), and learn more about promising regional and global practices. ADB staff should receive the training, guidance, and technical support they need to advise DMCs on non-infrastructure investments that can support CRPD implementation. Among these are investments in human resource capacity building, teacher training for inclusive education, community-based social services and rehabilitation for people with disabilities (including older people), attitudinal change, inclusive employment models, and private sector engagement—all tailored to individual country strategies (no "one size fits all" approach). Knowledge networks should be created, and disability champions or focal points identified, within ADB and across its various sectors, thematic groups, and regions.

1.6 **Update ADB operational guidance and tools** (2021–2025; STGs and BPMSD), especially where there are gaps in indicators and tools for gathering disaggregated disability data, but also in relation to poverty and social analyses, and consultations with people with disabilities during project planning and during implementation and monitoring. Safeguards and feedback loops for people with disabilities, and their implementation in the design of infrastructure and transport projects, should be strengthened.

Component 2: Establish strategic partnerships to leverage advocacy impact

2.1 **Map organizations of persons with disabilities that are active in the Asia and Pacific region** (2021; SDTG, NGO and Civil Society Center [NGOC]). CSO participation in ADB operations is being strengthened under the Deepening Civil Society Engagement for Development Effectiveness TA (ADB 2017b). Part of the support is focused on the mapping of CSOs, OPDs, and allied organizations (completed in October 2021). Through CSO focal points in selected DMCs, country-based solutions are being developed to enhance CSO engagement. This support also covers OP6 (strengthening governance and institutional capacity) of Strategy 2030, specifically in regard to citizen engagement.

2.2 **Engage with regional and global disability platforms and initiatives, and with civil society organizations** (2021–2025; STGs). ADB STGs will continue to bring new knowledge of regional challenges and progress in CRPD and Incheon Strategy implementation to the GLAD Network[15] and other platforms. At the same time, ADB will support its DMCs in accessing global knowledge or relevant resources pertaining to disability inclusion, in relation to the humanitarian response, gender, the private sector etc., through UNICEF, the Inclusive Education Initiative, the Global Partnership for Education, the Sustainable Mobility for All (SuM4All) initiative, the New Urban Agenda (Habitat III), and similar information sources (see Appendix 5 for examples of relevant global initiatives).

ADB is an active member of the GLAD Network and has established partnerships with CBM Australia,[16] for a better understanding of disability-inclusive development across ADB, and with the GDIH, for assistive technology, inclusive design, and inclusive education. In keeping with OP6 (strengthening governance and institutional capacity) of Strategy 2030, and with ADB's new policy of CSO contracting, engagement with OPDs and disability-oriented international NGOs and CSOs active in the region[17] and with initiatives such as the Paralympics and the Special Olympics are other ways of accessing knowledge and building ADB capacity for disability inclusion.

Consideration will also be given to engaging with other networks that can have an impact on disability-inclusive development across different sectors, such as the Global Social Service Workforce Alliance, national and regional professional associations of social workers and of health workers or rehabilitation health care providers, and professional associations in the fields of urban planning and road safety. Overall, ADB will seek to keep itself updated on the stakeholder landscape so that it can continually identify and engage with relevant actors.

2.3 **Advocate implementation of United Nations Convention on the Rights of Persons with Disabilities** (2021–2025). ADB should continue to participate in GLAD and other disability inclusion platforms, and through the Incheon Strategy and the Beijing Action Plan, promote CRPD implementation among government and other partners in the region during CPS and project planning. It should move away from medical models of disability and institutional rehabilitation and social care services and toward a bio-psychosocial and rights-based model of disability, universally accessible infrastructure and transport, community-based rehabilitation, social inclusion, inclusive education and employment, and independent living in the community for people with disabilities.

---

[15] The GLAD Network was launched in London in December 2015 by international financial institutions, bilateral agencies, the private sector, and foundations to realize the SDG promise that no one will be left behind, and to advance the principles reflected in the Convention on the Rights of Persons with Disabilities. These international development partners are working together to share expertise, coordinate actions, and raise the profile of disability.

[16] CBM is the disability inclusion advisory partner of DFAT. ADB has been partnering with CBM Australia via the support of DFAT (CBM Australia, n.d.). CBM is an international NGO specializing in disability-inclusive development worldwide. The name "CBM" originally stood for "Christian Blind Mission" in the early 20th century (CBM, n.d.[c]).

[17] For example, Humanity & Inclusion, Sightsavers, Helen Keller International, and Leonard Cheshire.

Component 3: Establish a culture of data collection and disaggregation, and publication of disability-sensitive analyses

3.1 **Analyze data on social protection coverage for persons with disabilities in the Asia and Pacific region, using ADB's social protection indicator database** (2021; SDTG). Analyses of social protection expenditure and coverage across countries in the region, with disaggregated data on disability as well as on age and gender, will generate new knowledge and understanding of the drivers of poverty and the barriers to inclusion for people with disabilities. The upcoming ADB reports on the Social Protection Indicator (SPI) for Asia and the Pacific include a special chapter with these analyses. The data provided will help in the monitoring of SDG indicator 1.3.1 (social protection coverage).

3.2 **Build ADB's capacity to address challenges in disability data disaggregation in its operations** (2021–2025). ADB staff should be provided with guidance and training in the use of Washington Group questions and other aspects of data strengthening systems to ensure the availability of disability-disaggregated data in ADB operations. Guidance and training should also be provided to the staff in the inclusion of people with disabilities and OPDs in project planning, implementation, and monitoring (including the strengthening of safeguards) and in the tallying and reporting of the number of people with disabilities participating in and benefiting from ADB investments.

3.3 **Generate new knowledge and regularly publish and update analyses of data** (2021–2025) on people with disabilities, aging, poverty, and gender in the Asia and Pacific region, based in the first instance on existing data and reports, and subsequently on the integrated safeguards monitoring system data that will emerge from strengthening safeguards.

Component 4: Develop sector guidelines and gradually expand the portfolio of disability-inclusive development interventions

4.1 **Infrastructure and urban development: Promote the use of ADB tool kits and provide guidance on accessibility and inclusion in the built environment** (2021–2025; Urban Sector Group and SDTG; Enabling Inclusive Cities Tool Kit for Inclusive Urban Development, 2017). Ways of documenting good practices in inclusive design guidance and in the creation of smart cities and sharing these within ADB should be developed to support all infrastructure projects and operations. These methods could involve consultations with people with all types of disabilities (including those with mobility, sensory, cognitive, and communication impairments; men and women; older people and young people; and parents of children with disabilities) during project planning, implementation, and evaluation. The links between disability and vulnerability to disasters and climate change should be taken into account in the preparation of guidance on planning and response to disasters and climate change, and the needs of people with disabilities should be considered in communications, search-and-rescue, and temporary shelter strategies and guidelines.

Support for the capacity building of the workforce in public administration, architecture, and construction management should be built into projects to help ensure the implementation of universal access regulations. Awareness should be developed, and support provided, for the improved availability and accessibility of information and communication facilities, including information and communication technologies and digital systems.

4.2 **Education: Identify gaps in the existing education portfolio** (2021–2025; Education Sector Group, SDTG) to further support inclusion and innovations that will expand the quality and range of disability-inclusive education policies, public finance mechanisms, and practices from early childhood development programs through kindergarten and pre-school, and the primary and secondary levels. These educational support mechanisms could include budgeting for teaching support resources in the classroom; building teacher competencies; developing national strategies for social and behavioral change to address stigma and other barriers to inclusive education in early childhood development programs and pre-school education; expanding the quality and range of accessible and disability-inclusive materials, teaching and learning approaches, and assistive devices and technology for learners with disabilities; and making the physical environment more accessible to these learners via universal design. The capacity of the education workforce at all levels of child education (early childhood, primary, secondary) should be developed. Ways of engaging students without disabilities in establishing an inclusive environment inside and outside the classroom (for example, teaching sign language to all students as well as teachers) should be identified. The Handbook on Poverty and Social Analysis includes tools for using communications for social and behavioral change to help address stigma.

4.3 **Education: Invest in accessible and disability-inclusive university degree courses, vocational training, and lifelong learning programs** (2021–2025; Education Sector Group, SDTG) to ensure the inclusion of people with disabilities. Investments should also be made in the capacity building of government and private academic and training institutions, the tertiary education workforce, and lifelong learning and adult education organizations, as well as in the development of inclusive policy and regulatory frameworks, finance mechanisms, programs for addressing stigma and supporting behavior change among teachers and peers, accessible buildings, and reasonable accommodation with assistive technology and mobility devices.

4.4 **Health: Incorporate disability inclusion in universal health coverage strategies** (2021–2025; Health Sector Group, SDTG) and in health sector reforms and the design of hospitals and health care facilities of the future. Measures that will expand national health insurance financing (and other types of government financing) for rehabilitation, mental health, prosthetics, assistive devices, and technology should be explored and promoted. Disability-inclusive post-COVID-19 response and recovery programs should be ensured. The capacity of the health sector workforce for disability inclusion and support for people with disabilities should be improved; all aspects of health care provision, such as sexual and reproductive health issues of women with disabilities, should be included. Knowledge of the relationship between noncommunicable diseases (NCDs) and disability, and of how interventions to prevent NCDs should also address disability inclusion, should be developed.

4.5 **Finance: Explore the possibility of introducing disability insurance** (2021–2023; Finance Sector Group, SDTG). New research into inclusive insurance, planned for 2022, will also provide important new insights into options for overcoming social exclusion and addressing poverty among people with disabilities in the region. ADB's Finance Sector Group (FSG) recognizes the importance of inclusive design and assistive technology for inclusive finance and will explore ways of strengthening disability-inclusive finance in collaboration with the research and development team of ADB's Information Technology Department and with the support of GDIH. The FSG is also aware of the need to develop sectoral guidelines on disability-inclusive finance.

4.6 **Private sector: Review disability-inclusive development and private sector linkages** (2021–2025; Private Sector Operations Department, SDTG) at the national, regional, and global levels, to identify entry points and opportunities to leverage disability-inclusive development impact from private sector operations.

4.7   **Social development: Continue to expand and promote a range of affordable and accessible community-based support and care services for children and adults, including older adults with disabilities** (2021–2025; operations departments, SDTG, GETG), ensuring their choice and control over where to live and which services to use. These efforts should include a focus on active aging, and cover support for independent living, community-based assistance to older people and adults with disabilities, and early intervention and care for children. ADB should continue to explore and promote inclusive employment practices and policies, taking into consideration the opportunities offered by digitalization of work. It should look into opportunities for collaboration to develop and scale up innovative service models, and to strengthen the regional knowledge base on the enabling environment required for service expansion, including financing; workforce development in the employment, health, education, and social sectors; quality management; and policy and regulatory frameworks. Recognizing the challenges of women and girls with disabilities, ADB should develop guidelines on gender and disability inclusion.

4.8   **Support disability-inclusive social protection** (2021–2025; SDTG, operations departments). More inclusive social protection will be pursued further under the new social protection strategic framework. In support of the COVID-19 recovery, gaps and design issues in social protection programs will be addressed, increasing the coverage of specific vulnerable groups, such as persons with disabilities.

4.9   **Build understanding of assistive technology and inclusive design** (2021–2025; SDTG and Urban Sector Group [USG]). A knowledge base on assistive technology and inclusive design, including barriers, challenges, and innovative solutions in financing, policy development, manufacturing, and design and implementation, should be developed in partnership with GDIH and other specialists. The Inclusive Design Bootcamp and the accompanying guidance notes, prepared with TA support from SDTG and USG, are expected to contribute to the development of sector guidelines (ADB 2019b, 2019d).

4.10   **Work toward supporting the developing member countries in implementing the United Nations Convention on the Rights of Persons with Disabilities in ADB-funded programs and projects** (2021–2025; STGs, operations departments)—inclusive and livable cities, accessible transport, elderly care, inclusive education and employment policies and practice, inclusive microfinance and livelihoods, supported independent living, accessible social protection and social insurance, inclusive financial services, inclusive health services, inclusive disaster and emergency preparedness and response, inclusive COVID-19 response and recovery with accessible communications and outreach—and moving away from medical models of disability. Regional frameworks for accelerating CRPD implementation, such as the Incheon Strategy and the Beijing Action Plan, set clear goals, targets, and indicators for most governments in the Asia and Pacific region and offer entry points for ADB support for disability-inclusive programs and projects. Identifying and amplifying flagship disability-inclusive projects and programs can spotlight how ADB can promote disability-inclusive development in its operations.

4.11   **Continue to track disability-inclusive operations in the corporate results framework, using the ADB disability inclusion marker system** (2021–2025; SDCC, Strategy, Policy, and Partnerships Department, operations departments). Pilot testing of the system is due to be finalized in 2021. Internal and external consultations are set to be conducted, and guidance and training in the use of the marker system will be rolled out to all staff in 2022–2023. The review of reports and recommendations of the President (RRPs) and other project design documents for the pilot testing of the corporate disability inclusion indicator and marker system will also provide new insights into the links between ADB business processes and opportunities for disability inclusion.

Component 5: Strengthen disability inclusion standards in the ADB workplace, and in its policies and practices

5.1   **Develop a Diversity, Inclusion, and Belonging Framework** (2021; BPMSD). Once the framework has been developed, a gap analysis will identify goals and specific actions to further strengthen ADB policies and practices. These actions could include developing an approach to reasonable accommodation and enabling staff with disabilities to self-identify if they are willing to do so. BPMSD and SDTG will work on raising awareness internally, for example, by supporting the observance of the International Day of Persons with Disabilities on 3 December each year and working with the Department of Communications to ensure that corporate language is aligned with the CRPD and with international best practice on disability, gender-responsiveness, and aging, as well as with other aspects of inclusion, such as meeting web accessibility guidelines. Other actions could involve seeking opportunities to create a more accessible and inclusive workplace environment by ensuring live signing at ADB events and closed captioning at online meetings. Specific actions and commitments will be fully defined after the benchmarking exercise.

5.2   **Include disability inclusiveness in sustainable procurement and training at ADB** (2021–2023; PPFD/SDCC). Disability inclusion, especially inclusive design, the needs of people with disabilities, and consultation with people with disabilities, should be considered in the guidelines on sustainable procurement used in ADB sovereign operations. PPFD will also support SDTG, the Urban Sector Group, and other parts of the organization in collating and promoting in training programs case studies where inclusive design or other disability inclusion principles have been included among the evaluation criteria for selecting contractors and awarding ADB contracts (by 2023).

Options for Providing Adequate Resources for Capacity Building

Lack of internal technical capacity for disability inclusion across sectors, thematic groups, operational departments, and country offices is one of the biggest challenges identified during preparations for the development of the road map. Strategies such as building internal capacity for disability-inclusive development, bringing in expert knowledge through technical assistance, developing effective external partnerships, and eventually hiring experienced staff are all required if ADB is to move forward across all five components and all priority actions of the road map.

ADB has some resources to support disability inclusion but no dedicated cross-sector expertise. Technical experts in social development, gender, and community development at ADB headquarters currently lead disability-inclusive development across the organization as part of a busy thematic portfolio. The urban development and transport sector teams also have expertise in universal design and inclusive urban planning, and the education sector team has experience and expertise in inclusive education and training programs. The health team at the Mongolia country office manage the Mongolia loan project Ensuring Inclusiveness and Service Delivery for Persons with Disabilities (ADB 2017a), but the project is intrinsically cross-sector, with components relevant to accessibility of community centers, social protection, inclusive employment, early childhood development, social development and social services, awareness raising, and gender.

Careful consideration should be given to options for building understanding, awareness, and technical capacity across sectors and across countries as ADB moves forward with the implementation of this road map for disability-inclusive development to achieve Strategy 2030 goals. The "One ADB" approach set out in Strategy 2030 will support the cross-sector, silo-breaking actions needed for effective disability-inclusive development. To build understanding, awareness, and capacity across sectors and across countries in preparation for the implementation of this road map, dedicated expertise could be created to support the capacity building of teams and the provision of technical assistance. The role of CPS leads could also be expanded to include explicit networking with OPDs and their inclusion in CPS and other consultations and ADB events; TA grants and projects with specific disability inclusion components; and ongoing and capacity building at ADB headquarters by CBM, GDIH, and other organizations. The nomination of disability focal points in country offices is likewise being considered, but this move should not prevent staff from building knowledge and understanding of disability-inclusive development on their own.

Monitoring and Evaluation

A foundation should be created for identifying indicators and informing a monitoring and evaluation plan, as well as for systematically building in-house technical capacity and understanding. Consolidating readily available data, reports, and knowledge will help in establishing this foundation. The disability reference group to be formed under priority action 1.2 will also have an important role in shaping the ADB model of disability-inclusive development and identifying indicators for the monitoring and assessment of road map implementation, in addition to the corporate disability inclusion indicator that is now being introduced. The monitoring and assessment plan for road map implementation will therefore be finalized only after the reference group has been formed and consulted on this framework and a plan has been drawn up for gathering and analyzing disability-disaggregated data across ADB programs and operations.

A midterm review of road map implementation will be commissioned, with the reference group taking part in defining the terms of reference and reviewing findings together with the evaluation team. A final evaluation will generate learning and recommendations for the next steps toward mainstreaming disability-inclusive development as an important central pillar of social inclusion and development in the post-2030 ADB organizational strategy.

The Way Forward

In the long term, ADB can work toward improved readiness to implement a strategic approach that strengthens disability inclusion across operations and programs, employment practices, and human resource management processes within the organization, while at the same time continuing to develop and invest in targeted programs benefiting people with disabilities and focused on eliminating specific barriers to inclusion. In the short to medium term, the commitments made at the Global Disability Summit in 2018 were a starting point for developing the building blocks for strengthening disability inclusion. Additional steps toward disability inclusion can be taken once capacity has been built and experience gained from the actions outlined above.

To achieve the core goals of Strategy 2030 of eradicating the remaining extreme poverty and achieving prosperity, inclusion, resilience, and sustainability, it will be important to keep a focus on achieving the empowered participation of persons with disabilities in the project cycle (planning, implementation, and monitoring and evaluation) across all sectors, as well as on ensuring that these persons benefit from ADB investments.

The review process for the monitoring and evaluation of progress in implementing this road map will offer an opportunity to set out goals for the next stage in the strengthening of disability inclusion.

Summary of the Proposed ADB Road Map for Disability-Inclusive Development

This road map is intended to support the implementation of Strategy 2030 across several priority operational goals and to enhance its impact on the poorest and most excluded populations in the region. It builds on ADB's strengths as a strategic regional expert investor and partner and on its experience in social inclusion, social development, gender mainstreaming, and disability-inclusive development.

Small, low-cost, quick-win steps are proposed as immediate priorities, with the active participation and empowerment of people with disabilities and the building of staff capacity and knowledge as core components. These steps will lay the foundation for building toward a more comprehensive and integrated disability-inclusive development approach in the medium to long term (see Appendix 1 for an overview of the key components and actions set out in the road map and the way in which these will be monitored and followed up).

The overall goal of this road map is to establish a more systematic approach to implementing disability-inclusive development in ADB, starting in 2021. The road map focuses specifically on short- and medium-term actions, across five core priority components, to introduce disability-inclusive development approaches and instill an inclusive organizational culture that can accelerate and strengthen the implementation of Strategy 2030 goals and priority areas.

Road Map Component	Key Actions	Responsible Department	Deliverables and Target Dates
1. Coordinate action on disability inclusion across ADB departments and sectors, and develop organizational capacity for disability-inclusive development	1.1 Finalize the road map	SDTG	1.1 Road map (to be approved after internal and external consultations in 2021 and annual consultation meetings)
	1.2 Develop guidance on disability-inclusive development	SDTG	1.2 Disability Brief, including case studies of ADB project experience with DMCs on disability inclusion (2022)
	1.3 Develop guidance on the corporate disability inclusion indicator and marker system	SPRA, SDTG	1.3a Disability indicator methodology guidance note (to be finalized by the end of 2021) 1.3b Results of 2020 review published (in annual DEfR report 2021); results of 2021 and future reviews published (in DEfR report 2022 and subsequent DEfR reports) 1.3c Staff consultation on the disability inclusion indicator methodology (2021/2022)
	1.4 Identify and engage with a disability inclusion reference group	SDTG	1.4 Annual meetings of reference group to review progress of actions and identify new actions (provide linkages with ESCAP country reviews) (2022–2025)

continued on next page

Table *continued*

Road Map Component	Key Actions	Responsible Department	Deliverables and Target Dates
	1.5 Build internal capacity and knowledge among ADB staff	SDTG	1.5a Management webinar on inclusive disability (CBM) (2021/22) 1.5b Inclusive Design Bootcamp (GDIH) (2021) 1.5c Annual capacity-building plan on disability inclusion for ADB staff and DMCs
	1.6 Update ADB operational guidance and tools	SDTG SDES	1.6a Updated Poverty and Social Analysis Handbook (2021–2022) 1.6b SPS policy update assessment on addressing disability inclusion (2021–2022) 1.6c Strengthened safeguard guidance (2023)
2. Establish strategic partnerships to leverage impact	2.1 Map OPDs through CSO focals in selected DMCs; develop country-based solutions to enhance CSO engagement	NGOC/SDTG	2.1a Report on mapping of OPDs (by September 2021) 2.1b Country-based engagement with OPDs in DMCs where CSO focals are active (2022–2025)
	2.2 Engage with regional and global disability platforms and initiatives	SDTG	2.2a Participation in GLAD meetings 2.2b Participation in ESCAP regional meetings
	2.3 Advocate CRPD implementation	SDTG	2.3 Ongoing, within guidance and training activities
3. Establish a culture of data collection and disaggregation, and publication of disability-sensitive analysis, involving people with disability in co-generation of data to help in understanding and contextualizing their experience	3.1 Build ADB operational capacity to address challenges in disability data disaggregation	SDTG/ERCD	3.1 Guidance and training in the use of Washington Group questions, for project staff (2022)
	3.2 Generate new knowledge on disability inclusion and regularly publish and update analysis		3.2 GDIH study on disability inclusion in primary education in Bangladesh and Mongolia (2022)
4. Develop sector guidelines and gradually expand portfolio of disability-inclusive development interventions	4.1 Infrastructure and urban development: Promote ADB tool kits and guidance on inclusive built environment	SDTG/EdSG, USG, SDCD	2021–2025
	4.2 Education: Identify gaps in existing education portfolio	EdSG	2021–2025
	4.3 Education: Invest in accessible university degree courses, vocational training, and lifelong learning programs	EdSG	2021–2025
	4.4 Health: Incorporate disability inclusion in universal health coverage strategies	HSG	2021–2025

continued on next page

Table *continued*

Road Map Component	Key Actions	Responsible Department	Deliverables and Target Dates
	4.5 Finance: Explore the introduction of disability insurance	FSG	2021–2023
	4.6 Private sector: Review disability-inclusive development and private sector linkages	PSOD	2021–2025
	4.7 Social development: Support community-based support and care services for children and adults; inclusive employment; SPI analysis	SDTG GETG	SPI chapter on disability (2021) Gender and disability guidelines (2022–2023)
	4.8 Adopt disability-inclusive assistive technology and inclusive design	SDTG/USG	2021–2025
	4.9 Adopt disability-inclusive social protection	SDTG	2021–2025
	4.10 Support DMCs in implementing CRPD in ADB-funded interventions	SDTG, with operations departments	2021–2025
	4.11 Track disability-inclusive operations in corporate results framework	OP1 monitoring team SPRA	Review of disability-inclusive operations Annual reporting in the DEfR on the number and % of operations that are disability-inclusive (also 1.3b)
5. Strengthen disability inclusion standards in ADB workplaces, policies, and practices	5.1 Draft and consult on a DIB framework within ADB	BPMSD	DIB framework (approved by the end of 2021) Gap analysis and benchmarking of disability inclusion at ADB, compared with other multi-donor banks and development organizations (2022–2023)
	5.2 Incorporate disability inclusion in the sustainable procurement guidelines	PPFD	Disability inclusion in sustainable procurement guidelines (2021) Support (from PPFD) and promotion of case studies on disability-inclusive procurement (case study preparation led by SDCC) from ADB sovereign operations in procurement training (2023)

ADB = Asian Development Bank; BPMSD = Budget, Personnel, and Management Systems Department (ADB); CRPD = UN Convention on the Rights of Persons with Disabilities; CSO = civil society organization; DEfR = Development Effectiveness Review; DIB = Diversity, Inclusion, and Belonging; DMC = developing member country; EdSG = Education Sector Group (ADB); ERCD= Economic Research and Regional Cooperation Department (ADB); ESCAP = United Nations Economic and Social Commission for Asia and the Pacific; FSG=Finance Sector Group (ADB); GDIH = Global Disability Innovation Hub; GETG = Gender Equality Thematic Group (ADB); HSG = Health Sector Group (ADB); NGOC = NGO and Civil Society Center (ADB); OPD = organization of persons with disabilities; PSOD= Private Sector Operations Department (ADB); SDCD = Climate Change and Disaster Risk Management Division (ADB); SDTG =Social Development Thematic Group (ADB); SPI = Social Protection Indicator; SPRA = Results Management and Aid Effectiveness Division (ADB); SPS = Safeguard Policy Statement; USG = Urban Sector Group (ADB).

APPENDIX 2
Summary of Donor Strategies

Summarized here are the donor strategies of the Foreign, Commonwealth & Development Office (FCDO, formerly DFID) of the United Kingdom, the World Bank Group (WBG), the Department of Foreign Affairs and Trade (DFAT) of Australia, and the Inter-American Development Bank (IDB).

Foreign, Commonwealth & Development Office (FCDO), UK

Key drivers, concepts, and definitions
- Exclusion drives poverty (DFID 2018a, 5)
- People with disabilities include people with mental health conditions, or psychosocial and intellectual disabilities (DFID, 2018a, 5)
- Social protection can take the form of social assistance such as cash transfers, social insurance, labor policies and standards, and social care (DFID 2018a, 9fn)
- Life-cycle approach, for all persons with disabilities, including psychosocial and intellectual disabilities (DFID 2018a, 13)

GDS2018 Charter for change	Goals and objectives
	• Ensure the rights, freedoms, dignity, and inclusion of all persons with disabilities.
	• Implement CRPD and deliver on SDG commitments relating to people with disabilities.

Influencing other donors (and CSOs and governments) through commitments to the following:
- Long-term planning, investment, and review
- Diverse representation of people with disabilities (of all ages)
- Legislation and policies to eliminate stigma and discrimination
- Inclusive, good-quality education (plans and resources)
- Economic and financial inclusion (more and better jobs, social protection, and employment for people with disabilities)
- Available and affordable assistive technology
- Inclusive and accessible humanitarian action
- Advocacy of the rights of the most marginalized people with disabilities of all ages, affected by multiple discrimination, especially girls and women with disabilities
- Collection and use of better data
- Self-accountability and the capacity to hold others accountable for their actions

Transparent publication of results achieved with respect to these commitments

FCDO's Strategy for Disability-Inclusive Development: Now Is the Time 2018–2023	Vision
	A world where no one is left behind. A world where all people with disabilities—women, men, girls, and boys—in all stages of their lives are engaged, empowered, and able to exercise and enjoy their rights on an equal basis with others, contributing to poverty reduction, peace, and stability.

continued on next page

Table continued

Strategic approach	Deliverables/Indicators
Seek outcomes and fundamental shifts through direct programs and leveraging of partnerships with other donors: • Human rights of people with disabilities fully recognized and respected • Full and active participation, representation, and leadership of people with disabilities—"nothing about us without us" • Equal access to opportunities and outcomes for all people with disabilities—universal design and built environment, access and affordability of assistive technology, adjustments and accommodations beyond physical barriers • Evidence-based understanding of exclusion related to disability—data and evidence on situations and barriers faced by people with disabilities and what works to improve outcomes **Four strategic pillars for action** • Inclusive education • Inclusive social protection • Economic empowerment • Humanitarian action **Three crosscutting areas consistently addressed in all work** • Tackling stigma and discrimination (through leadership of people with disabilities and OPDs, transformation of harmful stereotypes and unequal power relations, innovations tackling stigma, inclusive governance, and inclusive elections) • Empowering girls and women with disabilities • Improving access to technology and innovation **PLUS** Focus on mental health and well-being for people with disabilities, while also ensuring that disability inclusion programs are fully inclusive of people with psychosocial disabilities	**Pillar 1** • Translate policy (Get Children Learning) into action by leveraging international partnerships to invest in good teaching and back-system reform, and step up targeted support for the most marginalized. All school buildings funded by FCDO are accessible. • Increase the number of children with disabilities accessing inclusive and equitable good-quality education and improve learning outcomes through targeted interventions, especially for girls with disabilities. Providing counseling, mentoring, teacher training, and empowerment forums. • Catalyze will, tools, and resources to realize inclusive education (Inclusive Education Initiative, teacher reform, deinstitutionalized care and education for children with disabilities). **Pillar 2** • Engage in global advocacy of Global Disability Summit 2018 commitments. • Increase focus on disability-inclusive social protection. • Provide disaggregated data and better evidence base (using Washington Group questions on social protection monitoring and evaluation systems). **Pillar 3** • Address systemic and attitudinal barriers to economic empowerment by introducing and enforcing antidiscrimination laws and policies, modernizing the payment infrastructure, and improving access to financial services (e.g., through microfinance). • Enhance economic and social participation. Support people with disabilities as employers and employees and consumers. Engage with the private sector. Scale up access to jobs in manufacturing (through initiatives like Invest Africa). Disseminate good-practice notes on inclusive stability (in fragile and conflict-affected states). • Invest in accessibility and usability of infrastructure (including transport) and wider accommodations to give people with disabilities better access to economic opportunities. **Pillar 4** • Promote data disaggregation and improve the evidence base (all person-level data disaggregated by disability, by 2021). • Ensure equitable access to humanitarian services by conducting inclusion reviews to identify barriers, understand and share inclusive programming, and recommend improvements. • Advocate safety and protection of women, men, girls, and boys in humanitarian crises. All partners must demonstrate disability inclusion through disaggregated data and adhere to guidelines on gender-based violence. • Pursue reform of the international humanitarian system to effectively address disability inclusion by integrating system-wide guidelines, standards, and actions; holding partners to account; and strengthening collaboration with OPDs in humanitarian programming reforms.

continued on next page

Table *continued*

Implementation standards

- FCDO internal culture—disability champions in all business units; increased capacity to support employees with disabilities, and increased number of individuals with disabilities in the FCDO staff
- Engagement and empowerment of people with disabilities—through capacity building; inclusion of OPDs in full project cycle of design, implementation, and evaluation and in policy and strategy; and sufficient investments in OPDs to ensure meaningful engagement
- Influence on others—through regular engagement signaling the importance of disability inclusion, and support for governments in addressing stigma and discrimination
- Programming—needs of people with disabilities taken into account in all new business and annual reviews (marked with the disability and empowerment marker proposed by the Organisation for Economic Co-operation and Development and its Development Co-operation Directorate and Development Assistance Committee [OECD–DCD–DAC 2018]
- Data and evidence—systematic collection, use, and analysis of disability-disaggregated data using Washington Group questions
- "Living Our Values"—aim of having 19% of staff made up of persons with disabilities (same as working-age population); possibility of adjustments; inclusive procurement (DFID 2018a)

Monitoring and accountability

Disability Inclusion Delivery Board—senior officials from all relevant FCDO departments, who conduct quarterly reviews and assessments of progress and publish the findings in yearly reports
Independent Commission for Aid Impact—to conduct external scrutiny
FCDO progress report published November 2020: *Progress against DFID's Strategy for Disability Inclusive Development*

Learning

- Communities of practice in disability inclusion and mental health
- All DFID staff equipped with skills, tools, and knowledge to integrate disability inclusion into all policies and programs

Linked strategies and policies

DFID Education Policy (2018):
https://www.gov.uk/government/publications/dfid-education-policy-2018-get-children-learning

DFID Economic Development Strategy (2017):
https://www.gov.uk/government/publication/dfids-economic-development-strategy-2017

Age and Disability Capacity Programme, led by HelpAge International (see Age and Disability Consortium 2018, http://www.helpage.org/resources/publications/)

CRPD = United Nations Convention on the Rights of Persons with Disabilities, CSO = civil society organization, DFID = Department for International Development United Kingdom, FCDO = Foreign, Commonwealth & Development Office, OPD = organization of persons with disabilities.

World Bank Group

Key drivers, concepts, and definitions
50%–75% reduction in employment for people with disabilities
80% of people with disabilities living in developing countries
1/3 of 58 million out-of-school children having disabilities
Marginalization of persons with invisible disabilities
(World Bank 2018)

Disability and Inclusion Accountability Framework (Mcclain-Nhlapo et al. 2018). Multiple forms of exclusion, discrimination, and vulnerability arising from intersection of disability and gender, race, ethnicity, language, national or social origin, religion, age, sexual orientation, and gender identity, or other status (Mcclain-Nhlapo et al. 2018, 1)

People with disabilities among beneficiary groups in all World Bank projects (Mcclain-Nhlapo et al. 2018, 4). Disability-inclusive development facilitated through strong partnerships with governments, bilateral and multilateral development banks, and civil society, in particular, OPDs (Mcclain-Nhlapo et al., 2018, 4)

Disability-Inclusive Development Knowledge Silo Breaker, a network of staff members working on disability across the World Bank (Mcclain-Nhlapo et al. 2018, 9)

continued on next page

Table continued

World Bank Group	
Commitments on Disability-Inclusive Development	**With reference to CRPD implementation, SDGs, and the WBG Environmental and Social Framework**

- Inclusive education—(i) all education programs inclusive by 2025; (ii) host IEI (technical expertise and resources); (iii) private sector (principles of disability inclusion in education investments)
- Technology and innovation—(i) universal design and accessibility standards for all digital development projects (ICT-enabled services and resources, including promoting access to banking, health care, education, income generation, and government services); (ii) IFC to consider initiatives that could facilitate deployment of assistive technology emerging markets (new awards category)
- Data disaggregation—technical assistance and analytical support to scale up collection and effective use of disability data from national surveys and population censuses; inclusion of Washington Group questions in at least 50% of WBG-supported household surveys in LICs and LMICs from 2021; inclusion of profiles of disabled population in all publications
- Women and girls with disabilities—more deliberate focus on women and girls with disabilities
- Humanitarian contexts—universal design in public facilities in post-disaster reconstruction
- Transport—universal-access design features in all new public transport, urban mobility, and rail projects by 2025; equity considerations in SuM4All road map; advocacy of enhanced road safety (significant issues causing death and disability)
- Private sector—IFC to develop commitment on enhanced due diligence regarding disability inclusion and access
- Social protection—75% of social protection projects to be disability inclusive by 2025
- Staffing—increase in number of staff with disabilities in the WBG
- Disability Inclusion and Accountability Framework—promotion of framework among WB staff to support new ESF, which includes nondiscrimination provisions and requirements for stakeholder engagement

Strategic approach

Mainstream disability into WB activities, including policies, operations, and analytical work; build internal capacity to support clients in implementing DID programs
- Disability-inclusive development responds directly to WB goals of ending extreme poverty and promoting shared prosperity.
- This is a systematic and continuous approach to mainstreaming disability into operations to enable the effective participation of people with disabilities.
- The approach builds on WB role as a source of technical assistance for building know-how, and of evidence-based practices in implementing CRPD.

Six steps toward implementation
- Twin-track approach—(i) mainstreaming (people with disabilities participate in and benefit from all operations, projects, etc.); (ii) specifically targeted projects
- General policies—ESF, procurement, country engagement, M&E and reporting, accountability, and grievance resolution
- Focus areas for projects and advisory services—multisectoral and multidimensional approach across transport, urban development, resilience and disaster risk management, education, social protection, jobs and employment, ICT, water sector operations, and health care sectors
- Data collection—surveys; advisory services to client governments in census and household surveys to promote collection of disability-disaggregated data
- Internal capacity and assistance to clients—staff capacity and knowledge to be strengthened; Global Disability Advisor appointed
- Participation and partnerships to promote a cohesive and collaborative approach

Four guiding principles
- Nondiscrimination and equality
- Accessibility
- Inclusion and participation
- Partnership and collaboration

PLUS
Persons with invisible disabilities across all principles and steps

continued on next page

Table *continued*

World Bank Group
Linked strategies and policies
Environmental and Social Framework:
www.worldbank.org/en/projects-operations/environmental-and-social-framework

CRPD = United Nations Convention on the Rights of Persons with Disabilities, DID = disability-inclusive development, ESF = environmental and social framework, ICT = information and communication technology, IEI = inclusive education initiative, IFC = International Finance Corporation, LIC = low income country, LMIC = lower middle income country, M&E = monitoring and evaluation, OPD = organization of persons with disabilities, SDG = Sustainable Development Goal, Sum4All = Sustainable Mobility for All, WB = World Bank, WBG = World Bank Group.

Department of Foreign Affairs and Trade (DFAT), Australia

Key drivers, concepts, and definitions from Development for All strategy, 2015 and Disability Action Strategy, 2016 (DFAT 2015, DFAT 2016)

To be effective in reducing poverty, development must actively include and benefit people with disabilities (DFAT 2015, 6)
Disabilities = impairments + barriers (DFAT 2015, 6)

Disability-inclusive development promotes effective development by recognizing that, like all members of a population, people with disabilities are both beneficiaries and agents of development. An inclusive approach seeks to identify and address barriers that prevent people with disabilities from participating in and benefiting from development. The explicit inclusion of people with disabilities as active participants in development processes leads to broader benefits for families and communities, reduces the impact of poverty, and contributes positively to a country's economic growth. The prevention of impairments (for example, avoidable blindness and road safety activities) is outside the scope of disability-inclusive development in the Development for All strategy. (DFAT 2015, 9)

Disability inclusion within DFAT lends more credibility to the department's policies and advocacy of international disability issues (DFAT 2016)

Diversity and inclusivity are key to maintaining a modern, agile workforce (DFAT 2016)

Disability Action Strategy 2017–2020 (DAS)	**DFAT** aims to be an employer of choice for staff with disability, indeed, a model employer in the Australian Public Service

Innovations building on the previous DAS 2011–2015 have become business as usual:

- **Business as usual**

  Committed to employing more people with disabilities and promoting a culture that shares information about disability. DFAT Disability Network and Disability Champion. Disability confidence training provided by Australian Network on Disability. Mental Health First Aid and unconscious bias training for managers and staff. Improving responsiveness to requests for reasonable adjustments.

- **Immediate priority: becoming even more disability positive**

  Engaging actively with education providers to increase recruitment of graduates with disabilities. Improving career section of website to make it more accessible. Providing disability awareness training to all recruitment panels, new recruits, and people promoted to management positions. Improving access to assistive technologies across all information technology platforms.

- **Future goals and actions: enhance a culture that invests in and harnesses the attributes of all staff, including mature-age workers with disability**

  Reviewing the Reasonable Adjustment Policy. Advocating improvements in the metric used to measure the prevalence of disability in the Australian Public Service workforce. Advocating disability-inclusive clauses in aid contracts; examining feasibility of collecting disaggregated aid program data by age, gender, and disability; examining ways of improving disability inclusiveness in DFAT procurement; introducing a mechanism for measuring satisfaction with DFAT services as experienced by people with disability.

continued on next page

Table *continued*

Monitoring and accountability	
• DFAT Annual Report to Parliament • Australian Public Service Commission Annual State of the Service Report • Views of staff with disability, reported in the APS Employee Census	
Development for All 2015–2020 Strategy for strengthening disability-inclusive development in Australia's aid program (May 2015)	**Aid program goal:** sustainable economic growth and poverty reduction **Objective of disability-inclusive development:** improved quality of life for people with disabilities in developing countries • Enhancing participation and empowerment of people with disabilities as contributors, leaders, and decision makers in community, government, and the private sector • Reducing poverty among people with disabilities • Improving equality (of outcomes) for people with disabilities in all areas of public life, including service provision, education, and employment

Monitoring and accountability

- Monitoring of specific disability and poverty reduction targets in country and regional programs
- Monitoring, through the DFAT Disability Section, the overall performance of Australia's aid program in strengthening disability-inclusive development. Key indicators are the extent to which (i) barriers to inclusion and opportunities for participation have been identified and addressed; and (ii) OPDs have been involved in the project management cycle.
- Strategy midterm review and final evaluation
- Through the Disability Performance Assessment Note, provision of a range of indicators, guidance, and evaluative questions for program areas to draw from in designing disability-inclusive investments and M&E frameworks

Linked strategies, programs, and policies

Accessibility Design Guide: Universal Design Principles for Australia's Aid Program, 2013: https://www.dfat.gov.au/about-us/publications/Pages/accessibility-design-guide-universal-design-principles-for-australia-s-aid-program

DID4All: Resources for Disability Inclusive Development, with detailed evidence and guidance on mainstreaming disability-inclusive development into a range of sectors: https://www.did4all.com.au/

Inclusion Made Easy: A Quick Program Guide to Disability and Development, CBM's practical guide on ensuring that programs are disability inclusive, with basic inclusion principles, practical tips, and case studies: https://www.cbm.org/fileadmin/user_upload/Publications/cbm_inclusion_made_easy_a_quick_guide_to_disability_in_development.pdf

Australia–Indonesia Facility for Disaster Reduction
Australian Volunteers for International Development

CBM = Christian Blind Mission, DFAT = Department of Foreign Affairs and Trade Australia, OPD = organization of persons with disabilities.

continued on next page

Table *continued*

Inter-American Development Bank (IDB)	
Key drivers, concepts, and definitions	
The IDB prioritizes social inclusion and equality, to address the crosscutting issues of gender equality and diversity. The second update of the IDB Institutional Strategy confirms the importance of social inclusion and equality as one of three strategic priorities of the IDB Group in its work in Latin America and the Caribbean: https://www.iadb.org/en/about-us/strategies	
Commitments at the Global Disability Summit 2018	**Signing of the Summit Charter for Change** (see DFID, Government of Kenya, and IDA 2018) plus other commitments
<ul><li>Inclusive education—IDB committed to producing a sector note on disability and education to promote inclusive education in LAC; the Skills Development Sector Framework Document was published in 2020</li><li>Technology and innovation—IDB hosted a seminar on digital technology and disability inclusion at the IDB Multilateral Investment Fund Forum on Microenterprise in October 2018</li><li>Data disaggregation—IDB committed to supporting the collection of better disability data in the 2020 census round and is providing technical assistance to national statistics institutes</li><li>Women and girls with disabilities—IDB committed to producing a sector note on disability and violence against women, focusing on challenges and potential interventions in LAC https://publications.iadb.org/en/violence-against-women-and-girls-disabilities-latin-america-and-caribbean Violence against Women and Girls with Disabilities Latin America and the Caribbean was published in March 2019. The IDB has also committed to expanding its operational work to promote disability-inclusive development.</li></ul>	
Innovation and Creativity Division	Promotes social innovation for social change. Includes elements of communication for social change.
Strategic approach	
Crowdsourcing, participation, and social innovation	
Runs an initiative called I-Lab (https://www.bidinnovacion.org/en/), which holds periodic grant competitions to address social challenges. Projects related to disability-inclusive development have included: a 2012 call for proposals for innovative solutions and disruptive ideas for the labor market inclusion of people with disabilities: https://www.iadb.org/en/news/announcements/2012-09-25/i-lab-innovative-solutions-and-disruptive-ideas%2C10128.html	
Example of an inclusive education project using innovation and ICT: https://publications.iadb.org/bitstream/handle/11319/6639/CTI%20DP%20Social%20Innovation%20in%20Practice.pdf?sequence=1	
Linked strategies and policies	
Sector framework on gender and diversity: http://idbdocs.iadb.org/wsdocs/getdocument.aspx?docnum=39435256 Operational policies on gender equality and indigenous peoples: https://www.iadb.org/en/topics/gender-indigenous-peoples-and-african-descendants/idb-triples-loan-volume-in-two-years-for-programs-that-include-gender-results,7200.html	

DFID = Department for International Development United Kingdom, ICT = information and communication technology, IDB = Inter-American Development Bank, LAC = Latin America and the Caribbean.

Overview of ADB Disability Inclusion Indicator and Marker System

The Asian Development Bank (ADB) introduced an indicator into the Corporate Results Framework in 2019 in order to start tracking the extent to which ADB operations are disability inclusive. The corporate results framework indicator (ADB 2021c) reads as follows:

Disability-Inclusive Operations (%)
(Sovereign and Nonsovereign)

This is a proxy indicator related to SDG 10.

Number of committed sovereign and nonsovereign operations during the year that are disability inclusive, as a percentage of total number of ADB operations committed during the same period.

Operations are counted as disability inclusive if they are rated as: principally or significantly disability inclusive (rated 3); or, include some disability inclusion elements (rated 2).

ADB's methodology is based on the Organisation for Economic Co-operation and Development's disability marker and aligned with the United Nations Economic and Social Commission for Asia and the Pacific's 2012 Incheon Strategy and the 2017 Beijing Declaration and Action Plan to Accelerate the Implementation of the Incheon Strategy.

Cofinancing, investment facilities, revolving funds, transaction and knowledge and support technical assistance, and loans and grants supporting project preparation and design activities (SEFF activities) are excluded.

Frequency: Annual

ADB = Asian Development Bank, SDG = Sustainable Development Goal, SEFF = small expenditure financing facility.
Source: ADB data (SPD and SDCC).

A draft rating system for assessing whether a project is disability inclusive, designed following a review of international practice and aligned with the disability inclusion policy marker being developed by the Organisation for Economic Co-operation and Development (OECD) Development Assistance Committee, has been adopted by a number of development organizations including the Foreign, Commonwealth & Development Office (FCDO) of the United Kingdom (formerly the Department for International Development, or DFID) and the Department of Foreign Affairs and Trade (DFAT) of Australia. The ADB draft marker system is summarized in the table.

Proposed ADB Rating System for Disability Inclusion

Rating	Rating Description
3	Principally or significantly disability inclusive
2	Some disability inclusion elements
1	Enabling conditions for disability inclusion, no explicit disability inclusion elements
0	No disability inclusion, no enabling conditions for disability inclusion

Source: Asian Development Bank.

The draft ADB marker system has been adapted for use in ADB operations and in the regional disability inclusion framework, in recognition of the fact that the Incheon Strategy and the Beijing Action Plan provide a system of indicators and targets that are relevant to the governments in the region and that have been developed together with organizations of persons with disabilities (OPDs) in the region. Operations are considered disability inclusive if they are rated as: principally or significantly disability inclusive (rated 3) or include some disability inclusion elements (rated 2). Operations that only support or create the conditions for disability inclusion and have no explicit disability inclusion elements (rated 1) are excluded.

ADB operations are rated 3 (principally or significantly disability inclusive) if:

- people with disabilities or their representative organizations are explicitly involved in project design, monitoring, and implementation and benefit from the project;

AND

- the projects have explicit disability inclusion goals, outcomes, and disability-disaggregated data clearly indicates the distinct impact of the project activities on people with disabilities;

OR

- they result in substantial legislative, policy, or regulatory changes contributing to Incheon Strategy goals and targets or indicators;

OR

- they contribute substantially to achieving Incheon Strategy goals and targets or to implementing the Beijing Declaration and Action Plan as demonstrated by disability-disaggregated data.

ADB operations are rated 2 (some disability inclusion elements) if:

- the needs of people with different types of disabilities are explicitly considered in the planning stage and they are explicitly expected to form part of the target beneficiary group;

OR

- the operation provides explicit measures to ensure that people with disabilities will have access to the project benefits, and to measure the extent of access with the use of disability-disaggregated data;

AND

- the operation contributes at least to some extent to achieving Incheon Strategy goals and targets and/or to implementing the Beijing Declaration and Action Plan, as demonstrated by disability-disaggregated data.

ADB operations are rated 1 (having enabling conditions for disability inclusion, no disability inclusion) if:

- people with disabilities are mentioned as a distinct target group;

OR

- explicit measures supporting disability inclusion are described;

AND

- these projects contribute, at least to some extent, to achieving Incheon Strategy goals and targets.

In 2019, 146 approved projects were reviewed by means of this system and 5.5% of projects were assessed as being disability inclusive (8 projects rated 3 or 2) and 22% (32 projects rated 3, 2, or 1) were either disability inclusive OR enabling disability inclusion (Figure A3.1).[1]

Most of these (32 projects) were urban infrastructure or transport projects.

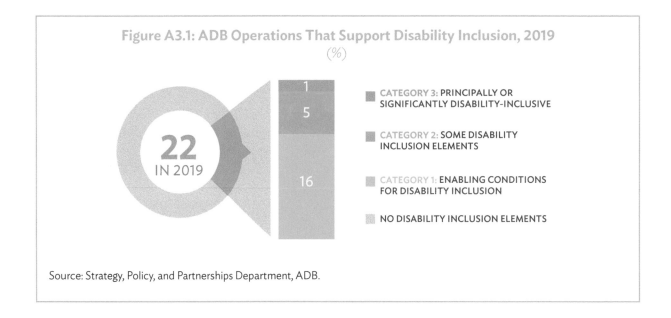

Figure A3.1: ADB Operations That Support Disability Inclusion, 2019
(%)

22 IN 2019

1
5
16

CATEGORY 3: PRINCIPALLY OR SIGNIFICANTLY DISABILITY-INCLUSIVE

CATEGORY 2: SOME DISABILITY INCLUSION ELEMENTS

CATEGORY 1: ENABLING CONDITIONS FOR DISABILITY INCLUSION

NO DISABILITY INCLUSION ELEMENTS

Source: Strategy, Policy, and Partnerships Department, ADB.

In 2020, 173 approved projects were reviewed with the help of this system. The scores were validated by ADB regional departments and project teams, which also provided additional information about the operations, leading in many cases to a higher score, especially for projects in category 1. **Eight percent of operations committed in 2020 were disability inclusive**—three operations (2%) were marked principally or significantly disability inclusive (rated 3) and eleven (6%) were marked as having some disability inclusion elements (rated 2). A further 41 operations were marked as category 1 (having enabling conditions for disability inclusion, no disability inclusion elements). Overall, 32% of committed operations in 2020 were rated disability inclusive or created enabling conditions for disability inclusion (Figure 2).

---

[1]   The first two pilot assessments covered 2019 and 2020 RRPs and used a scoring system with "2" as the highest level of disability inclusiveness, as reported in the Development Effectiveness Reviews of 2019 (ADB 2020b) and 2020 (ADB 2021a), and in alignment with the OECD system, where "2" is the highest score. The scoring system was adjusted following the second review. Now, projects in category 3 (formerly category 2) are those that are principally or significantly disability inclusive; projects in category 2 (formerly category 1A) have some disability inclusion elements; and category 1 projects (formerly 1B) create enabling conditions for disability inclusion but have no disability inclusion elements.

Figure A3.2: ADB Operations That Support Disability Inclusion, 2020
(%)

32
IN 2020

2

6

24

■ CATEGORY 3: PRINCIPALLY OR
SIGNIFICANTLY DISABILITY-INCLUSIVE

■ CATEGORY 2: SOME DISABILITY
INCLUSION ELEMENTS

■ CATEGORY 1: ENABLING CONDITIONS
FOR DISABILITY INCLUSION

■ NO DISABILITY INCLUSION ELEMENTS

Source: Strategy, Policy, and Review Department, ADB.

The **Mumbai Metro Railways System** project is an example of a project marked as significantly disability inclusive (rated 3) as it has the following disability-inclusive elements:

- Explicit representation of people with disabilities in consultations and focus group discussions;

- Design features on platforms, in ticket halls, and in carriages for people with disabilities;

- Disaggregated indicators specifying feedback from people with disabilities on the quality of the transport infrastructure; and

- Communications and staff training activities that aim to promote ease of access, safety, comfort, and other advantages, as well as "zero tolerance" for sexual and other forms of harassment experienced by people with disabilities (and also the older persons, and women and children).

Disability inclusion could be strengthened if:

- the project were to disaggregate people with disabilities more clearly from the generic group of beneficiaries considered "vulnerable"; and

- the project's impact were to be measured by a survey of 2,000 people and if this group were to include people with disabilities (not made clear in the report and recommendation of the President). A disability access audit conducted by people with different disabilities would further strengthen the project's disability inclusion rating.

The **Guizhou Gui'an New District New Urbanization Smart Transport System Development** has some disability inclusion elements, but these are much weaker than those in the Mumbai Metro project. It is therefore considered as rating 2 (having some disability inclusion elements). The project takes into account people with disabilities and their different needs and has explicit indicators for disability-accessible buses and bus stations. However, it does not engage with people with disabilities or explicitly target them.

Both of these projects contribute to Incheon goals on accessible infrastructure and transport.

The RRP and the design and monitoring framework (DMF) for many of the ADB road construction projects approved in 2019 mention that these projects have "safety and design features that are sensitive to the needs of women, children, elderly, and differently-abled people." These features, and the DMF indicator mentioning their inclusion, are enough to mark the projects as rating 1 (enabling disability inclusion). But lack of analysis and information about the people with disabilities who use the roads, and lack of consultation with people with disabilities and their representative organizations (OPDs), means that these projects cannot be considered disability inclusive (ratings 2 or 3).

A typical example is the **Public–Private Partnership in Madhya Pradesh Road Sector Project.** This project supports road infrastructure with features that are friendly to the elderly, women, children, and people with disabilities (EWCD), and the DMF has two indicators that are footnoted "with EWCD-friendly features and road safety measures at appropriate locations." These design considerations are almost an afterthought in the project RRP. While the project contributes to the Incheon target on accessible infrastructure, and so is considered category 1, there is no analysis of which people with disabilities might use these roads and safety features. Explicit consultation with OPDs and people with disabilities who are likely to use the road (including women with disabilities who are targeted by the gender mainstreaming measures and activities), both during design and as part of monitoring or feedback, and accessibility audits conducted among these potential road users would improve the project rating to category 2.

The marker system for measuring the corporate indicator for disability inclusion was developed and tested in 2020 and will be further refined and gradually rolled out in 2021–2025 (ADB 2021b).[2]

---

2   The details are available from ADB. Guidance Note on ADB's Disability Inclusion Indicator and Marker System. Unpublished.

Draft Terms of Reference for a Disability Inclusion Reference Group

Background

The Asian Development Bank (ADB) is working toward strengthening disability-inclusive development approaches across its operations by 2025. This *Road Map for Strengthening Disability-Inclusive Development, 2021–2025,* includes a range of activities from building staff capacity on disability through reviewing ADB data and reports for disability-disaggregated data and new knowledge about the situation of people with disabilities to promoting the design of disability-inclusive and disability-targeted programs in the Asia and Pacific region. The road map is intended to support the implementation of ADB's Strategy 2030 and its overall goals of reducing poverty and inequality in the region. ADB recognizes that these goals cannot be achieved without the explicit participation and targeting of people with disabilities, who are among the poorest and most excluded population groups across the region. ADB also recognizes the intersection of disability and age, gender, ethnicity, religion, and other drivers of inequality and exclusion.

Purpose of the Disability Inclusion Reference Group

ADB seeks to establish and engage with a disability inclusion reference group that can inform, shape, and validate its approach to strengthening disability-inclusive development across operations and help it to stay up-to-date and connected with relevant networks, initiatives, and resources in the region and globally. The main purpose of the reference group is to support the implementation of the ADB road map for disability-inclusive development and the participation of people with disabilities in informing, monitoring, and shaping disability-inclusive development in ADB.

Main Tasks of the Disability Inclusion Reference Group

- Review and approve the terms of reference, code of conduct, and meeting rules for the reference group at the first meeting.

- Meet periodically, review reports on the implementation of the road map and other relevant documents, and report against the Road Map Monitoring and Reporting Matrix.

- Provide comments and inputs to support a disability-inclusive approach and the implementation of the ADB Strategy 2030.

- Provide advice and information to ADB to help it stay up-to-date on what is happening in the region in regard to disability inclusion, and help it to connect with relevant networks, initiatives, and programs.

Criteria for Inclusion in the Reference Group

The individual:

- Is a representative of a national, regional, or international organization of persons with disabilities (OPD), as defined in General Comment No. 7 of the CRPD Committee (CRPD Committee 2018);[3] or

- Self-identifies as a person with disabilities and has experience of the societal barriers of living with a disability; or

- Is an academic or expert from member countries with expertise in disability-inclusive development and in a position to inform ADB strategy development, planning, monitoring, and review in terms of disability inclusion.

- Has a proven track record in disability-inclusive development in the Asia and Pacific region and a willingness to engage with ADB to inform, monitor, and validate its approach to disability inclusion.

The members of the reference group, taken together, should:

- Be at least 50% people with disabilities representing OPDs.

- Be 50% women.

- As far as possible, represent or have expertise relating to people with a range of different types of impairments, including intellectual disabilities, autistic spectrum disorders, mobility, sight and hearing impairments, etc.

- Have experience and expertise across a range of issues, services, methods, and approaches to implementing the CRPD and a disability-inclusive development approach—inclusive education, health and employment, independent living, legal advocacy, assistive devices and technology, universal design, accessible transport, participatory research and social action, inclusive financial and social protection policies and programs, disaster response, inclusive climate change response, advocacy on social inclusion and gender, communications, and other technical areas relevant to ADB operations.

- Be representative of a range of national, regional, and global experience, interests, and agendas concerning people with disabilities, including children and young people with disabilities, women with disabilities, and older people.

Inputs

Reference group members will serve as resource persons and provide periodic inputs over a 2- to 3-year period. ADB will take the necessary steps to ensure access and allow for full participation of all participants (accessibility, language and sign interpreters, braille versions of documents).

---

3   "The Committee considers that organizations of persons with disabilities should be rooted, committed to and fully respect the principles and rights recognized in the Convention. They can only be those that are led, directed and governed by persons with disabilities. A clear majority of their membership should be recruited among persons with disabilities themselves."

Examples of Global Initiatives and Frameworks Relevant to Supporting a Disability-Inclusive Development Approach

Sector/initiative
GLAD Network: www.gladnetwork.net
ESCAP: https://www.unescap.org/our-work/social-development/disability-inclusive-development
Education
GLAD working group on inclusive education
Inclusive Education Initiative: https://www.worldbank.org/en/topic/socialsustainability/brief/inclusive-education-initiative-transforming-education-for-children-with-disabilities
Global Partnership for Education: https://www.globalpartnership.org/
UNICEF Inclusive Education: https://www.unicef.org/education/inclusive-education
Economic (Private Sector)
IFC Performance Standards (and Good International Industry Practice, GIIP)
CDC group (UK government development finance institution)—will work with IFC to develop a Good Practice Note on Disability Inclusion
Mental Health
WHO Mental Health Action Plan
Women and Girls with Disabilities
UN Trust Fund for the Prevention of Violence against Women
Women Entrepreneurs Finance Initiative (We-Fi)
Humanitarian
IASC guidelines on disability inclusion + Humanitarian Inclusion Standards
Humanitarian Innovation and Evidence Program (HIEP)
Assistive technology and mobility devices
Global Partnership for Assistive Technology (ATscale): https://atscale2030.org
Sustainable Mobility for All initiative (SuM4All)
WHO Priority Assistive Products List https://www.who.int/publications/i/item/priority-assistive-products-list
Data
Washington Group questions: https://www.washingtongroup-disability.com

continued on next page

Table *continued*

Transport
Global Road Safety Facility: https://www.roadsafetyfacility.org
Built Environment
New Urban Agenda (Habitat III): https://www.un.org/sustainabledevelopment/blog/2016/10/newurbanagenda/
Disaster Risk Reduction
Sendai Framework: https://www.unisdr.org/we/coordinate/sendai-framework
Twin-Track Approach: Mainstreaming and Targeted Interventions
WHO, Community Based Rehabilitation Guidelines, 2010
OECD/DAC policy marker for disability-inclusive financing (2019): https://www.oecd.org/officialdocuments/publicdisplaydocumentpdf/?cote=DCD/DAC/STAT(2020)48&docLanguage=En

CDC = Colonial Development Corporation, GLAD = Global Action on Disability, ESCAP = United Nations Economic and Social Commission for Asia and the Pacific, IASC = Inter-Agency Standing Committee, IFC = International Finance Corporation, OECD DAC = Organisation for Economic Co-operation and Development Development Assistance Committee, UNICEF = United Nations Children's Fund, WHO = World Health Organization.

Glossary

Disability	A result of the interaction of long-term physical, mental, intellectual, or sensory impairments with various barriers (social, physical, communication, economic, attitudinal, behavioral) in the environment that constrains a person's full participation in society. (Based on the United Nations Convention on the Rights of Persons with Disabilities, or CRPD)
People with disabilities	People with long-term physical, mental, intellectual, or sensory impairments, which, in interaction with various barriers, may hinder their full and effective participation in society on an equal basis with others. (Based on the CRPD)
Children with disabilities	Human beings under 18 years of age who have long-term physical, mental, intellectual, or sensory impairments, which, in interaction with various barriers, may hinder their full and effective participation in society on an equal basis with others. (Based on the CRPD and the United Nations Convention on the Rights of the Child)
Organizations of persons with disabilities	Organizations that are "led, directed and governed by persons with disabilities" (as defined in General Comment No. 7 of the CRPD Committee), with a majority of members recruited among persons with disabilities.
Reasonable accommodation	"Necessary and appropriate modification and adjustments not imposing a disproportionate or undue burden" (as defined in Article II of the CRPD). Reasonable accommodation enables people with disabilities to participate on an equal basis by making adjustments, which may include, but are not limited to, the environment, process, schedule, equipment, and provision of assistance.

References

Age and Disability Consortium. 2018. *Humanitarian Inclusion Standards for Older People and People with Disabilities.* Under the Age and Disability Capacity Programme (ADCAP) of the consortium, which comprises CBM, DisasterReady.org, Handicap International, HelpAge International, the International Federation of Red Cross and Red Cross Societies, Oxford Brookes University, and RedR UK.

Alisjahbana, A. S. 2020. Empowering the Disabled in a Post-COVID World. *Nikkei Asia.* 2 December.

Asian Development Bank (ADB). 2005. *Disability Brief. Identifying and Addressing the Needs of Disabled People.* Manila.

————. 2012. *Handbook on Poverty and Social Analysis: A Working Document.* Manila.

————. 2014. *Guidance Note: Poverty and Social Dimensions in Urban Projects.* Manila.

————. 2016. *Enabling Inclusive Cities: Tool Kit for Inclusive Urban Development.* Manila.

————. 2017a. *Report and Recommendation of the President to the Board of Directors: Proposed Loan and Administration of Grant to Mongolia for the Ensuring Inclusiveness and Service Delivery for Persons with Disabilities Project.* Manila.

————. 2017b. *Technical Assistance for Deepening Civil Society Engagement for Development Effectiveness.* Manila.

————. 2018. ADB Reaffirms Commitment to Support People with Disabilities in Asia. Manila.

————. 2019a. *Living with Disability in Mongolia: Progress toward Inclusion.* Manila.

————. 2019b. *Technical Assistance for Integrated and Innovative Solutions for More Livable Cities.* Manila.

————. 2019c. *Technical Assistance for Strengthening Safeguards implementation in ADB Projects.* Manila.

————. 2019d. *Technical Assistance for Supporting the Operational Priority 1 Agenda: Strengthening Poverty and Social Analysis.* Manila.

————. 2020a. *COVID-19 and Livable Cities in Asia and the Pacific: Guidance Note.* Manila.

————. 2020b. *Development Effectiveness Review 2019.* Manila.

————. 2021a. *Development Effectiveness Review 2020.* Manila.

———. 2021b. *Tracking Indicator Definitions*. Manila.

———. Forthcoming. *Briefing on Disability*.

———. Forthcoming. *Social Protection Indicator Report* (Asia).

———. Forthcoming. *Social Protection Indicator Report* (Pacific).

———. Guidance Note on ADB's Disability Inclusion Indicator and Marker System. Unpublished.

Astbury, J., and F. Walji. 2013. *Triple Jeopardy: Gender-Based Violence and Human Rights Violations Experienced by Women with Disabilities in Cambodia*. AusAID Research Working Paper 1. January. Canberra.

Australian Network on Disability. n.d. Business Benefits of Employing People with Disability (accessed May 2016). Sydney.

Buckup, S. 2009. *The Price of Exclusion: The Economic Consequences of Excluding People with Disabilities from the World of Work*. Employment Working Paper No. 43. 14 December. Geneva: International Labour Organization (ILO).

CBM. 2016. *Inclusion Counts: The Economic Case for Disability-Inclusive Development*. Bensheim, Germany.

———. 2017. *Disability-Inclusive Development Toolkit*. Bensheim, Germany.

———. n.d.[a]. Disability and Climate Change: Understanding Vulnerability and Building Resilience in a Changing World. Bensheim, Germany.

———. n.d.[b]. Disability Inclusive Development (DID). Bensheim, Germany.

———. n.d.[c]. https://www.cbm.org/

CBM Australia. n.d. https://www.cbm.org.au/.

Department of Foreign Affairs and Trade (DFAT), Australia. 2015. *Development for All 2015–2020: Strategy for Strengthening Disability-Inclusive Development in Australia's Aid Program*. Extended to 2021. Canberra.

———. 2016. *Disability Action Strategy 2017–2020*. Canberra.

Department for International Development (DFID), UK. 2018a. *DFID's Strategy for Disability Inclusive Development 2018-23*. London. https://assets.publishing.service.gov.uk/government/uploads/system/uploads/attachment_data/file/760997/Disability-Inclusion-Strategy.pdf.

———. 2018b. *Education Policy 2018: Get Children Learning*. London. https://www.gov.uk/government/publications/dfid-education-policy-2018-get-children-learning.

———. 2018c. Minimum and High Achievement Disability Inclusion Business Standards for Each DFID Business Unit. London.

Department for International Development (DFID), UK; Government of Kenya; and International Disability Alliance (IDA). 2018. *Global Disability Summit 2018 Charter for Change.* London.

Diversity Council Australia. n.d. Business Case: Disability & Accessibility (accessed May 2016).

Dunkle, K., I. van der Heijden, E. Stern, and E. Chirwa. 2018. *Disability and Violence against Women and Girls: Emerging Evidence from the What Works to Prevent Violence against Women and Girls Global Programme.* London: UK Aid.

Foreign, Commonwealth & Development Office (FCDO), UK. 2020. *FCDO Disability Update: Progress against DFID's Strategy for Disability Inclusive Development.* London.

Governance and Social Development Resource Centre (GSDRC), UK. 2015. Poverty and Disability. University of Birmingham.

HelpAge International. 2015. *Global AgeWatch Index 2015: Insight Report, Summary and Methodology.* London.

HelpAge International and the American Association of Retired Persons (AARP). 2018. *Global AgeWatch Insights: The Right to Health for Older People, the Right to Be Counted.* London.

Inclusive Futures. 2020. *The Impacts of COVID-19 on People with Disabilities: A Rapid Review.* Report prepared with funding from the UK Department for International Development under the Disability Inclusive Development Programme. Bristol, England.

International Labour Organization (ILO). n.d. World Social Protection Data Dashboards. https://www.social-protection.org/gimi/WSPDB.action?id=19.

Mont, D. 2007. *Measuring Disability Prevalence.* Social Protection Discussion Paper No. 0706. March. Washington, DC: World Bank.

Morgon Banks, L., and S. Pollack. 2014. *The Economic Costs of Exclusion and Gains of Inclusion of People with Disabilities: Evidence from Low and Middle Income Countries.* International Centre for Evidence in Disability, London School of Hygiene & Tropical Medicine.

Office of the United Nations High Commissioner for Human Rights (OHCHR). 2020. *Policy Guidelines for Inclusive Sustainable Development Goals.* Geneva.

Organisation for Economic Co-operation and Development (OECD). 2018. *Proposal to Introduce a Policy Marker in the CRS to Track Development Finance that Promotes the Inclusion and Empowerment of Persons with Disabilities.* Paris.

Ortoleva, S., and H. Lewis. 2012. *Forgotten Sisters—A Report on Violence against Women with Disabilities: An Overview of Its Nature, Scope, Causes and Consequences.* Northeastern University School of Law Research Paper No. 104-2012. 21 August. Boston.

Spratt, J. M. 2013. *A Deeper Silence: The Unheard Experiences of Women with Disabilities—Sexual and Reproductive Health and Violence against Women in Kiribati, Solomon Islands and Tonga.* Suva, Fiji: United Nations Population Fund Pacific Sub-Regional Office.

Uji, K., and H. Björkman. 2021. Improving Accessibility for People with Disabilities—A Neglected Priority in the Response to COVID. 20 May. UNDP Bangkok Regional Hub.

United Nations. 2008. *United Nations Convention on the Rights of Persons with Disabilities (CRPD)*. New York. https://www.un.org/development/desa/disabilities/convention-on-the-rights-of-persons-with-disabilities.html.

———. 2019. *Disability Inclusion Strategy*. New York.

———. 2021. United Nations Convention on the Rights of Persons with Disabilities (CRPD): Ratification Status, as of November 2021. New York.

———. n.d. Disability-Inclusive Sustainable Development Goals: 2030 Agenda for Sustainable Development. New York. https://www.un.org/disabilities/documents/sdgs/disability_inclusive_sdgs.pdf.

United Nations Children's Fund (UNICEF). 2017. Inclusive Education. New York. https://www.unicef.org/eca/sites/unicef.org.eca/files/IE_summary_accessible_220917_brief.pdf.

United Nations Children's Fund East Asia and Pacific Regional Office (UNICEF EAPRO). 2020. *Education for Every Ability: A Review and Roadmap of Disability-Inclusive Education in East Asia and Pacific Region.* Bangkok.

United Nations Convention on the Rights of Persons with Disabilities (CRPD) Committee. 2015. General Comment No. 3 on Women with Disabilities. *United Nations Convention on the Rights of Persons with Disabilities.* Geneva.

———. 2018. General Comment No. 7 on the Participation of Persons with Disabilities, in the Implementation and Monitoring of the Convention. Section II, A.11. Geneva.

———. 2021. UN Treaty Body Database. https://tbinternet.ohchr.org/_layouts/treatybodyexternal/TBSearch.aspx?Lang=en&TreatyID=4&DocTypeID=29.

United Nations Department of Economic and Social Affairs (UN DESA). 2020. *Leaving No One Behind: The COVID-19 Crisis through the Disability and Gender Lens.* Policy Brief No. 69. New York. https://www.un.org/development/desa/dpad/publication/un-desa-policy-brief-69-leaving-no-one-behind-the-covid-19-crisis-through-the-disability-and-gender-lens/.

United Nations Department of Economic and Social Affairs (UN DESA) / Population Division. 2017. *World Population Prospects: The 2017 Revision—Key Findings and Advance Tables.* New York.

United Nations Development Programme (UNDP). 2014. *The State of Human Development in the Pacific: A Report on Vulnerability and Exclusion in a Time of Rapid Change.* Report prepared in association with the United Nations Population Fund (UNFPA), the United Nations Economic and Social Commission for Asia and the Pacific (ESCAP), the United Nations Children's Fund (UNICEF), and the International Labour Organization (ILO). Suva, Fiji.

United Nations Economic and Social Commission for Asia and the Pacific (ESCAP). 2012. *Incheon Strategy to "Make the Right Real" for People with Disabilities in Asia and the Pacific.* Bangkok.

———. 2017. *Disability in Asia and the Pacific: The Facts—2017 Midpoint Review Edition.* Policy brief. 8 December. Bangkok. https://www.unescap.org/sites/default/d8files/knowledge-products/Disability_The_Facts_2.pdf.

———. 2018a. Incheon Strategy to "Make the Right Real" for Persons with Disabilities in Asia and the Pacific and *Beijing Declaration, Including the Action Plan to Accelerate the Implementation of the Incheon Strategy.* Bangkok.

———. 2018b. *Building Disability-Inclusive Societies in Asia and the Pacific: Assessing Progress of the Incheon Strategy.* Bangkok.

———. 2019a. *Disability at a Glance 2019: Investing in Accessibility in Asia and the Pacific— Strategic Approaches to Achieving Disability-Inclusive Sustainable Development.* Bangkok.

———. 2019b. *Report on the Fifth Session of the Working Group on the Asian and Pacific Decade of Persons with Disabilities, 2013–2011.* 21–22 February. Bangkok.

———. n.d. *Ensuring Disability Rights and Inclusion in the Response to COVID-19.* Policy brief. Bangkok.

United Nations Educational, Scientific, and Cultural Organization (UNESCO). 2018. *Education and Disability: Analysis of Data for Asia-Pacific Countries.* Paris.

United Nations General Assembly. 2019. *Report of the Special Rapporteur on the Rights of Persons with Disabilities.* A/74/186. July. New York.

United Nations Office for the Coordination of Human Affairs (OCHA). 2020. Disability Considerations in GBV Programming during the COVID-19 Pandemic. Istanbul, Turkey.

United Nations Office for Disaster Risk Reduction (UNDRR). 2015. *Sendai Framework for Disaster Risk Reduction 2015–2030.* Geneva.

United Nations Population Fund (UNFPA) Asia-Pacific Regional Office. n.d. https://asiapacific.unfpa.org/.

Washington Group on Disability Statistics. 2016. The Washington Group / UNICEF Child Functioning Module (CFM). University College London.

———. n.d. Washington Group on Disability Statistics.

World Bank. 2018. World Bank Group Commitments on Disability-Inclusive Development.

World Health Organization. 2021a. Rehabilitation 2030 Initiative. Geneva.

———. 2021b. WHO Disability Assessment Schedule 2.0 (WHODAS 2.0). Geneva.

Lightning Source UK Ltd.
Milton Keynes UK
UKHW051236010822
406663UK00005B/126

9 789292 693763